For Reitu,

An old school hand,

Ruth

Winter 2014

"Forward and No Retreat"
Two Centuries of Linsly School Life

by
Richard Hawley

Publication of this history of
The Linsly School
is made possible through the support of the
ELIZABETH STIFEL KLINE FOUNDATION
(John C. W. Kline, John C. Harmon, and WesBanco Bank, Trustees)
in loving memory of its founder
Elizabeth Stifel Kline;
her parents, Henry G. Stifel, Sr., and Elizabeth Stevenson Stifel;
her grandparents, Louis Carl Stifel and Elizabeth Stamm Stifel;
and
her great-grandparents, Johann Ludwig ("J. L.") Stifel and Barbara Becht Stifel,
a family of Wheeling industrialists and philanthropists
for over 175 years.

Copyright © The Linsly School

ISBNs: 978-0-692-25794-4

Library of Congress Control Number: 2014946430

All Rights Reserved. No part of this book may be reproduced or transmitted in any form or by any means, electronic or mechanical, including photocopying, recording, or by any information storage and retrieval system without written permission from the author, except for the inclusion of brief quotations in a review.

Printed in the United States of America.

This book is dedicated to the boys and girls of The Linsly School—and to the men and women they will become.

Table of Contents

Author's Preface vii

1. The Two Noahs. 1
2. The Linsly Institute: A New Mission. 7
3. The Great War and a Determination to Serve 13
4. A Greater Linsly 19
5. Enduring the Great Depression 26
6. The War Years 32
7. Linsly at Mid-Century 37
8. The Challenges of "The Sixties" Era 48
9. A New Direction: The Arrival of Headmaster DiOrio 56
10. The Road to Coeducation 63
11. A New Coherence: Linsly Through the Nineties 71
12. Linsly On Course 85
13. Linsly at Two Hundred 105

Note on Bibliography and Sources 117
Faculty and Staff for 2013-14 & 2014-15 School Years 200th Anniversary Celebration 121
Index 127
Author Biography 131

Author's Preface

A VISITOR APPROACHING THE LINSLY SCHOOL FROM THE EAST OR WEST WILL EXIT Interstate 70 in Wheeling, West Virginia, and proceed for less than a mile on the National Road past low-slung auto service shops, fast-food eateries, and other strip retail establishments. A small, easy-to-miss circular sign bearing the school's name in orange and black directs one down Leatherwood Lane to what seems an unlikely prospect. Opening up before one is the pleasingly settled campus—dormitories, classroom buildings, playing fields—of Linsly. The school's sixty-five acres rise in graduated tiers from the margin of Wheeling Creek to the hillside residences overlooking Knox Lane.

The first time I visited Linsly I was struck by how quickly I had seemed to change worlds from the traffic and strip retail below to what could only be a school. Even now, after many visits, the drive up Leatherwood Lane seems to carry me out of the workaday world into a better, highly purposeful one.

When the longtime Linsly headmaster, Reno DiOrio, now serving the school as president, contacted me in the summer of 2012 about possibly writing a history of the school to help commemorate its bicentennial, I was not sure I could do it. The two prior school histories I had written were of the University School in Cleveland and the Kiski School in Saltsburg, Pennsylvania. I had taught at the University School for twenty years before I composed that history and then went on to be its headmaster; I felt I knew the school in my bones. I did not know Kiski as well, but it was far from unfamiliar. Kiski had over the years become a respected athletic rival in our Interstate Prep School League (IPSL), a consortium that also included the Cranbrook School in Detroit; the Nichols School in Buffalo, New York; Shady Side Academy in Pittsburgh, the Western Reserve Academy in Hudson, Ohio; and, beginning in 1980, Linsly. As headmaster, I had also enjoyed a close personal friendship with Kiski's iconic headmaster of forty-six years, Jack Pidgeon. By contrast, Linsly was largely unexplored territory. I had met—and liked—Reno DiOrio years ago when he was the assistant headmaster of Kiski. In his early years as Linsly's headmaster, he had invited me to the school to address his faculty and student body about a variety of educational issues. But whether in just a year I could learn enough to write a useful history—two hundred years of it, no less—gave me pause.

Ultimately what persuaded me to take on the job, in addition to the graciousness of the invitation, was the challenge of getting to know a school and a region to which I had so little prior exposure. But beyond the challenge, I also had a hunch. My single prior visit and impressions gathered from football and basketball games between the University School and visiting Linsly teams somehow planted the notion in me that there was more to the place than the larger world, including the independent school world, might imagine. And in that hunch my research during this past year has proven to be absolutely correct.

Moreover—and this is not always the case when institutional histories are commissioned—Linsly's history has genuine story quality. In the 200 years since Noah Linsly's will set it in motion, the school has proceeded adaptively forward through a succession of nearly ruinous challenges without retreat. In 1832 Wheeling was ravaged by an epic Ohio River flood that carried a good deal of the city's infrastructure away while submerging most of Wheeling Island. The following year a deadly cholera epidemic decimated so many Wheeling citizens—including Noah Linsly's best friend and the fledgling school's early champion, Noah Zane—that the dead lay in heaps too numerous to be buried. And while the city would rebound and even gain renown as the nation's Gateway to the West, the economic panic of 1873, brought on by the collapse of the silver standard for currency and a succession of national disasters across the country, stalled the regional economy to the crisis point. Similarly, when the Great Depression of the 1930s brought the nation's economy to its knees, coal and steel-based cities like Pittsburgh and Wheeling were the most deeply affected. The Second World War would fortify the school's military mission, but the antiwar sentiment unleashed during the Vietnam era, combined with a surge of youth-driven challenges to traditional schooling, created a climate in which a fee-charging military institute might no longer be sustainable.

Yet the school Noah Linsly projected to serve his adopted city would not only endure these crises, but also emerge from them stronger, with renewed resolve—and often substantially transformed. Linsly alumnus and past archivist Robert Schramm (1952) has documented that Linsly was but one of eighteen independent academies chartered in what is now West Virginia between the late seventeenth and early eighteenth century. Linsly is the only one to have endured. The school today is in fact the state's oldest school of any kind in continuous operation. Three factors appear to be at work in this remarkable achievement: the vision to discern when structural change was necessary; the periodic arrival of strong, dedicated, and long-serving school leaders; and an extraordinary tenacity in the face of hardship, a quality foreseen in Noah Linsly's will when he charged his school to proceed ever "forward and no retreat."

Except for its continuing commitment to serve the children of Wheeling and beyond, the school has been remarkably adaptive. The rigorous and decorous college preparatory school of today would certainly have surprised—and

Author's Preface

probably pleased—Noah Linsly, who set out to establish what was then a rising educational innovation: a Lancastrian Academy, designed to serve poor boys and girls otherwise unlikely to be schooled at all. The Lancastrian approach, transported to the early republic from England, was part of a progressive child-centered educational movement embraced later by Maria Montessori. In the mid-nineteenth century, when Wheeling began to offer free schools to its children, the Lancastrian Academy modified itself to become an "institute" offering advanced and classical studies that would qualify graduates for university admission, if they so chose, and for the professions. When sisters of the Catholic Visitation Order established a new school for girls in 1852, the Wheeling Female Academy, enlarged in handsome new surroundings in 1865 as Mount de Chantal, the institute responded by becoming an all-boys school in 1861. At the conclusion of the Civil War, for which so many of its recent graduates had trained to serve, Linsly formally became a military institute, a proud and defining tradition it would retain for more than a century until irrepressible cultural developments following the Vietnam War persuaded the school's trustees to terminate the military program (1978) and to proceed as a traditional college preparatory school. In 1988, The Linsly School joined the ranks of the majority of American independent schools by once again admitting girls.

Guiding the school through these protean transformations was a succession of dedicated school leaders. Whether due to pestilence, economic hardship, or changing cultural attitudes, Linsly hovered several times at the brink of collapse or assimilation into the city's public schools. At each crisis point, the presiding trustees refused to abandon the enterprise, and a visionary school leader emerged to build enrollment and to strengthen the scholastic program. In the mid-nineteenth century the school's course was righted when the Rev. John Scott established a classically rigorous and otherwise rich scholastic program before moving on to become president of Washington & Jefferson College. After the Civil War John Michael Birch would lead the school to regional prominence, his terms of service broken up first by a call to establish a public high school for Wheeling, then to serve the U.S. embassy in Japan. In 1910 he was called out of retirement to help the school restore its badly flagging enrollment. Birch died at his post in 1911.

Prior to America's entry into the First World War, the youthful Guy Holden had established himself as a charismatic young teacher and coach. After the war, Lieutenant Holden returned, literally, to the cheers of his former students and colleagues. Appointed principal of the institute in 1919, Holden presided over a growing school until the impact of the Depression in the 1930s once again seriously threatened the school's viability. Holden met the challenge by a series of imaginative improvisations, including first halving and then eliminating his own salary. For these generous gestures and for his tireless recruiting of prospective students over a decade in which few families in the region had enough marginal income to afford the school's modest fees, Holden has rightly been proclaimed "the man who saved Linsly."

As the Depression eased at the close of the decade, Holden, who would not live another year, confided to his trustees that he had made the strongest faculty hire in the past quarter century, Basil Lockhart. Lockhart, with his newly acquired master's degree from West Virginia University, would succeed Holden as principal in 1939 and guide the school through a period of remarkable physical expansion, including the establishment of the boarding program. Lockhart led the school with a firm hand for thirty-three years. When he stepped down in 1972, the baby boomers conceived after World War II had begun to make a distinct cultural impact. For the first time in American history there were more people under than over twenty-five years old. The cultural historian Theodore Roszak dubbed the era the "Adolescentization of America." Born into unprecedented affluence, the surge of baby boomers tended to press limits and to demand more personal freedom and mobility. First the nation's colleges, then its schools began to confront the demands of student bodies who felt empowered to speak out, demonstrate, and sometimes obstruct standard scholastic business. The Linsly Institute, with its military program and otherwise decorous tradition, would not be undone by the more extreme youthful challenges of the period, but in the late sixties and early seventies, all the school's constituents—students, parents, faculty, trustees—contended with the question of whether an all-boys military program provided the best preparation for the world as it had become and, more practically, whether such a program was sustainable.

When, after protracted deliberations, the institute's trustees voted to terminate the military program in December 1978, there was considerable uncertainty as to what of the old Linsly might remain and what lay ahead. The uncertainty was heightened by a succession of three headmasters in just six years. When Board Chairman Don Hofreuter announced the appointment of Reno DiOrio, the youthful yet seasoned assistant headmaster of the Kiski School in Saltsburg, Pennsylvania, as the first headmaster to lead the school in its post-military mode, anticipation ran high. With DiOrio's arrival clarity was restored to the school's mission and tone. The tradition of student leadership was largely retained through a melding of merit-based military rankings into a prefectorial system. Required military dress was replaced with traditional school uniforms, including school blazers and ties. Linsly's trademark scholastic rigor and athleticism continued apace, and the school's enrollment steadily grew. Like Holden and Lockhart before him, DiOrio would see the school through both challenges and encouraging growth, including, in 1988, the successful transition—a reversion, in Linsly's case—to coeducation. Holding fast to the "forward and no retreat" spirit in which the school was founded, DiOrio's thirty-year tenure as headmaster was characterized by the motto "Never, never, never quit."

Author's Preface

When Headmaster Chad Barnett, who had led the school since 2009, announced in the autumn of 2013 that he would be leaving Linsly to serve as headmaster of St. Edmund's Academy in Pittsburgh, the school approached its bicentennial year once again on the threshold of change. Enjoying full enrollment and a strong scholastic program supported by a seasoned and dedicated faculty, Linsly's passage into its third century of continuous operation would be an occasion for both celebration and high hopes.

However the interwoven trajectories of the school and the city of Wheeling have waxed and waned, both have found adaptive means to move forward, with no retreat. Wheeling as of this writing is a city of a little over 28,000, its population having declined annually from a peak of 61,000 in 1930. The city and region have rebounded before. For decades after its resurgence in the early nineteenth century, Wheeling and the National Road it helped to develop was the nation's Gateway to the West. When the French hero of the American Revolution, the Marquis de Lafayette, returned to the young republic in 1825 to be honored for his contribution to American independence, he made it a point to stop in Wheeling where he raised a toast the city's bright future.

In a similar spirit a century later, Charles Lindbergh included Wheeling in his triumphant flying tour across the country in the aftermath of his historic transatlantic flight. Greeted by what local journalists estimated to be 100,000 well-wishers from the region, Lindbergh found time to make his way to Linsly's Thedah Place campus where he placed a wreath at the foot of Augustus Lukeman's timeless sculpture, *The Aviator*.

Apart from being a national "destination," Wheeling has periodically made its mark on the larger culture. For more than a century after its founding in 1840, the Marsh Wheeling cigar company's stogies were the signature cigar of the United States. The lock gates that opened the historic Panama Canal to international commerce in 1914 were fashioned by Wheeling's Mold and Foundry.

Today, Wheeling and the surrounding region sit atop the heart of the Marcellus Shale, a geological formation spanning much of Appalachia, including Pennsylvania, West Virginia, and Ohio. The shale contains enough untapped natural gas, speculators believe, to advance the United States to energy self-sufficiency. If environmentally feasible, tapping the new fuel and transporting it to refineries could provide an economically bracing infusion of new infrastructure and employment.

Whatever the impact of such developments may be for Wheeling and its surroundings, there is little doubt that a rigorous and spirited independent school will be on hand to serve willing and qualified boys and girls—a school propelled "forward and no retreat" by two centuries of momentum.

RAH
Ripton, Vermont

1 | The Two Noahs

The Linsly School, now entering its third century of continuous operation, and the city of Wheeling, West Virginia, quite literally grew up together. The best historical guess is that *Wheeling* was an Anglicized approximation of a native Lenni-Lenape term roughly translated as "place of the head." Oral tradition indicates that the head in question was that of a European frontiersman who attempted to settle on the promising bottomland where the present-day Wheeling Creek joins the Ohio River. The unlucky pioneer was decapitated by Iroquois natives who displayed the severed head on a pike to discourage future trespassers.

Such obstacles to further settlement did not deter the enterprising Ebenezer Zane (1747–1811) from establishing in 1769 "tomahawk rights"—a process consisting of killing a stand of trees near a spring, removing the bark, and inscribing the initials of the prospective settler into the wood—to "the place of the head." When sufficient land was cleared and a residence constructed, Zane brought his wife, brothers, and sister to live in the settlement they would call Zanesburg. The Zanes would be joined soon after by other founding Wheeling families, including the Shepherds, Wetzels, and McCullochs.

Not surprisingly, the Shawnee and other Ohio Valley tribes contested the European incursion. Early skirmishes convinced Ebenezer Zane, who had served as an officer first in the Crown's and then in Virginia's own colonial militia, that the Wheeling settlement would not survive without fortified military protection. A delegation of militia from Fort Pitt in Pennsylvania was dispatched to Wheeling in 1774 to build what was briefly Fort Fincastle in honor of the colonial governor of Virginia, Viscount Fincastle, Lord Dunmore, but as revolutionary tensions mounted between Crown and colony, the fort's name was changed to Fort Henry in recognition of Virginia patriot Patrick Henry.

Fort Henry would prove to be the Wheeling settlement's salvation. Throughout the 1770s and early 1780s Shawnee, Wyandot, and Mingo tribes attacked frontier settlements along the Ohio River, and while Fort Henry, often under siege, enabled the Zanes and their fellow settlers to survive, their homes, crops, and outbuildings were periodically burned and razed. Throughout the course of the Revolution (1776–82), British troops were allied with Ohio Valley tribes to weaken the colonies' western defenses.

During this period Fort Henry was the scene of two legendary events in Wheeling lore. The first, "McColloch's leap," celebrates the narrow escape in 1777 of Ebenezer Zane's brother-in-law, Major Samuel McColloch, from a pursuing band of Shawnee. McColloch, while leading mounted reinforcements to Fort Henry from a nearby fort, was separated from his party by the attacking Indians. Chased to the precipitous rim of Wheeling Hill, McColloch and his horse leaped to what his attackers believed to be his certain death, but when they gained the edge of the precipice, they peered down to see McColloch three hundred feet below them, galloping safely off to Fort Henry.

In 1782 Fort Henry was again besieged, this time by allied Indian and British forces. The defenders had run out of gunpowder and were on the brink of defeat when Zane's sister Elizabeth ("Betty") volunteered to make a dash to the family homestead where additional powder was stored. According to early accounts she was heckled by both soldiers and Indians as she ran to the house, but was fired upon and nearly hit when she ran back to the fort bearing a tablecloth full of powder. Her heroics enabled Fort Henry to withstand the siege in what some historians have determined to be the last North American battle of the Revolutionary War.

One of the victorious survivors of the siege was Ebenezer Zane's four-year-old son, Noah (1778–1833), who would go on to become the cofounder of the Linsly School. While Noah's father continued after the war to advance his scheme of building a "national road" westward into Ohio territory and beyond, Noah would remain in Wheeling as first citizen and civic visionary. Resting on the bank of a great navigable river, connected already by a good road to commercial supplies as far east as Baltimore, and with a newly passable track—"Zane's trace"—into developable land in Ohio and beyond, Wheeling stood poised to become what would in just a few decades be called the young republic's Gateway to the West.

By the close of the eighteenth century Wheeling had grown to more than three hundred residences and twelve hundred people, and prospects for further growth were limitless—or so it seemed to another Noah, Noah Linsly, who set up residence in Wheeling in 1799. Like Noah Zane, two years his junior and soon to become his closest friend, Noah Linsly was a man of parts.

Born in 1772 in Bradford, Connecticut, Linsly would go on to study at Yale where he earned his BA degree in 1791. After a brief period teaching at what is now Williams College in Williamstown, Massachusetts, Linsly went on to earn MA degrees from both Williams and Yale. In 1797 he migrated to Morgantown in what was still western Virginia in order to establish a law practice, which did not prosper. Reckoning that his prospects might be brighter closer to the frontier, he resettled in Wheeling in 1799.

In the years remaining to him Linsly thrived in Wheeling. By 1804 he had parlayed his legal practice into an appointment as Commonwealth Attorney for the region. Soon after his arrival he became a member of the Wheeling Town Council, and between 1810 and 1814 served as the town's fourth mayor. In his civic duties he would of course work closely with Noah Zane, who became his closest friend. Contemporaries described Linsly as a tall man of ruddy complexion, dignified in bearing and nattily turned out. He never married. In 1813 a deadly scourge Wheeling residents called "the cold plague" infected a number of townspeople including Linsly, who developed tubercular symptoms and died of a lung hemorrhage the following year.

Just forty-two when he died, Linsly had earlier shared with Noah Zane his vision of a new, progressive school for the town. In his will of March 2, 1814, Linsly bequeathed his treasured Yale ring to Zane, along with instructions to apply money from his estate to establish a "Lancastrian Academy" for the purpose of educating at no cost Wheeling's "poor White Children [sic]." Not only did Linsly have in mind a highly specific and progressive model for the new school, he declared that its "Guiding Principle" must be "Forward and no Retreat." Linsly closed his will with an affectionate tribute to his fellow townsmen in Wheeling including, cryptically, his desire to "leave memorys [sic] of what is not yet to Come." Central to those memories not yet to come was the emergence of The Linsly School, the two-hundred-year trajectory of which would have astonished and most likely delighted its founder.

Chartered formally as The Lancastrian Academy by the Virginia legislature in 1814, the school was reflexively associated with Noah Linsly by the locals, so that whether constituted formally over the years as an "academy," "institute," or "school" it was most commonly referred to as "Linsly," with spelling variations ranging from "Linsley" to "Lindsley." While the nation's founders, Jefferson foremost among them, had stressed the crucial role an educated citizenry must play in a participatory democracy, it is nonetheless remarkable that such a progressive educational notion as a *Lancastrian Academy* would take root in a frontier outpost like Wheeling. But as a scholar at Yale and then a teacher in Williamstown, Linsly had apparently given considerable thought to how schools operate and, more tellingly, how children actually learn.

At the time the new school was chartered in Wheeling, the Lancastrian method, sometimes called the Bell-Lancastrian method, was just beginning to transform public thinking about elementary education, first in England and then the United States. Two British educational theorists, Andrew Bell and Joseph Lancaster, both committed to teaching all children at public expense, arrived independently at similar approaches to mass education. Through a combination of effective public speaking and the establishment of a number of new schools modeling their principles, Bell and Lancaster anticipated many of the developmental, "child-centered" elements championed decades later by Rudolf Steiner's Waldorf Schools and Maria Montessori's schools. Like Montessori, Lancaster's aim was to educate all children, including the poorest of the poor.

Structurally, Lancastrian schools and classrooms were to be built to exact specifications, so that adequate ventilation, natural light, and teachers' and children's access to one other could be assured. Children in the equivalent of today's primary grades would master the alphabet and basic writing by inscribing letters and words in sand tables positioned at the outer margins of the instructional space. The schools would serve all children, although boys and girls would be physically separated on opposing sides of the classroom; on playgrounds, a fence was to separate the sexes. Character development was promoted through a series of graduated honors and prizes for commendable behavior, reprimands and deprivations for unacceptable behavior. Lancaster was a Quaker and forbade any form of physical punishment.

Bell and Lancaster proposed that the expense of mass education could be greatly reduced if older, more accomplished children were enlisted as "monitors" to instruct and supervise younger ones. Lancastrians believed that, with the aid of student monitors, a hundred children might be productively engaged in schoolwork under the supervision of a single adult teacher.

Such was the theoretical vision Noah Zane sought to realize as he proceeded after his friend's death to procure a school charter from the Virginia legislature (1814), then to recruit a board of trustees, of which he was elected president at its inaugural meeting in May 1815. Zane donated two lots at the corner of what are now Thirteenth and Chapline Streets in Wheeling to house the completed school building. It would be nearly five years before sufficient funds were raised to build the original schoolhouse, a two-story brick building constructed approximately along the lines Lancaster proposed.

In its early years few records were preserved indicating the number and ages of the students enrolled. The academy was presided over by a single teacher, John F. Truax, who served for seven years before heading off to seek more lucrative employment. While there is no record of how much of the school's modest endowment was set aside to pay its teacher, it was apparently not enough to sustain a long-term commitment. Truax's successor, Daniel Deady, served only a year, followed by Alexander McGee, who departed after two. In his pictorial history of the school composed in 2003 Robert Schramm (1952) speculated that the short tenure of the school's first teachers may have been attributable to the daunting range of their assigned duties. In addition to teaching all children all subjects, the head teacher was required to maintain the building, repair breakage, and whitewash the walls.

Under the watch of the academy's next lead teacher, Thomas Lees (1830–46), the fledgling school would grow considerably in the course of a substantial boom in Wheeling's population. Due both to the completion in 1818 of the National Road linking Cumberland, Maryland, to Wheeling and to lively speculation in land and minerals in the region, the city's population had swelled to over 5,000 residents by 1830. Indeed, Wheeling had become something of a "destination."

Such was the opinion of none other than Marie-Joseph Paul Yves Roch Gilbert du Motier, Marquis de Lafayette—General Lafayette—a hero of the American Revolution who at age nineteen, against the wishes of France's *ancien régime*, made his way to the colonies to serve as major general under George Washington. The dashing young general, who had volunteered to serve without pay, rendered admirable service in campaigns spanning the Brandywine battles of 1777 to the decisive siege of Yorktown in 1781. Lafayette had been a passionate advocate for the American cause to a French regime skeptical of provoking England. On May 24, 1825, the sixty-eight-year-old Lafayette, his son George Washington Lafayette, and a suitable entourage arrived in Wheeling aboard the river steamer *Herald* as part of a triumphant return tour of the country he had helped to create.

By all published accounts, Lafayette's ceremonial visit to Wheeling was a signal moment in the history of the city. A local broadsheet proclaimed, "All the beauty, fashion, and intellect of Wheeling had assembled to witness the imposing scene." Citizens lined the streets between the dock and Simm's Hotel downtown. Seated beside the general in the open carriage was his host Noah Zane, who recounted the civic developments in Wheeling since the revolution. The entourage was escorted along the parade route by a unit of western Virginia's "Independent Blues" in full dress. After an extended banquet during which the general's achievements were warmly celebrated, Lafayette returned the favor, toasting the assembled diners with "Wheeling! Center of communication of the East and the West!" An audience of well-wishers afterward included "many a hoary veteran" who, one local journalist wrote, "pressed around [Lafayette and] eagerly grasped the hand of his loved, but long-absent commander."

In a note composed the following June thanking Zane for his accommodations in Wheeling, Lafayette wrote, "I shall never forget to be escorted up your Main Street with you Noah under the military escort from The Lancastrian Academy." Zane had apparently waxed eloquently on the promise of the new school, which at that time had no military program, confusing the general.

Gratifying as such a civic celebration may have been for the residents of the growing city, both Wheeling and the Lancastrian Academy would be gravely challenged in the decade ahead. An especially severe Ohio River flood in 1832 damaged a great deal of property and civic infrastructure, temporally submerging Wheeling Island and destroying most of its buildings. The following year, 1833, brought more deadly devastation in the form of an extended epidemic of cholera, believed to have been carried to Wheeling through its steamboat commerce. Mortality was severe and unabated for more than a year, straining the city's ability to dispose of its corpses. Contemporary accounts remarked on the grim spectacle of coffins piled up at the entrance of Greenwood Cemetery awaiting available manpower to bury them. City officials mandated every known measure to curb or slow the infection, including treating cellars and waste with lime. Perhaps unwisely, the town fathers prohibited the sale of fruits and vegetables. Coal fires were tended on street corners in the belief that the sulfur fumes would kill the cholera germs.

The yearlong epidemic all but brought the city to its knees. Few households were spared the loss of at least one family member. So many families fled the region that an article in *The Wheeling Times* reported the unnerving spectacle of once teeming streets barren of pedestrians and vehicles. On New Year's Day, 1834, the paper printed a poem composed by the Lancastrian Academy's head teacher, Thomas Lees, attempting to express the depth of his city's and his school's loss.

> *Rank pestilence went forth by night and day*
> *Sweeping our race like autumn leaves away.*
> *Death bared its weapon with terrific might,*
> *And all was desolate, fear and fright;*
> *All human schemes, all projects at an end;*
> *No power on earth could mortal man defend;*
> *His haughty spirit humbled to the dust*
> *Sought in Omnipotence its only trust:*
> *All else was perilous beneath the sky,*
> *'Twas death to tarry and 'twas death to fly…*

While Lees himself would survive the scourge, many of the children in his charge either died or fled the city with their families. By the time the epidemic receded in the summer of 1834, an estimated 50 to 60 percent of the population had died. One of those deeply mourned was Noah Zane, who succumbed in the autumn of 1833.

The city would languish for several years in the economic depression that followed the epidemic. Now lacking the guidance of its champion and virtual founder Noah Zane, the academy teetered on the brink of closure. This was due in part to a growing momentum nationwide to establish a uniform system of public education, a movement that would triumph in the coming decade under the banner of Horace Mann's Common School Movement. The mounting appeal of state-provided education coincided with waning enthusiasm, both in England and America, for the Lancastrian system, which, critics claimed, produced no observable advantage over other approaches. In 1833, the year of the cholera outbreak, the academy's board of trustees recorded being approached on three occasions to combine with the newly established free public schools. The proposals were rejected, but in the decade to follow, the declining school would struggle to sustain itself.

2 | The Linsly Institute: A New Mission

As Wheeling began to recover its population and economic vitality over the course of the 1840s, the school was faced with a series of challenges that would ultimately enlarge its original mission of serving the city's "poor white children." By 1835 the founding trustees of the academy had, like Zane, either died or moved on. For a period of ten years there are no records of trustee activity until John McClure emerged as trustee president in 1845. McClure reconstituted the role of lead teacher to "principal," a post first held by the Rev. John W. Scott, who from 1847 and 1852 led the school, now generally referred to as Linsly (or Linsley) Institute, back to sustainable enrollments.

Nevertheless, at mid-century the academy's prospects were not promising. Wheeling's publicly supported free schools were now fully functioning and thus enrolling boys and girls who might otherwise have been candidates for Linsly. The pool of potential students was reduced further when, in 1848, a Catholic delegation of sisters from the Visitation Order in Baltimore established what would become in 1852 the Wheeling Female Academy. The new girl's school flourished to the point that by 1865 a handsome, new neo-Gothic facility was erected on Washington Avenue, on a site designated as Mount de Chantal. Renamed Mount de Chantal Visitation Academy, the school would enroll Wheeling-area girls until it closed its doors in 2008.

Further threatening the viability of what the *Wheeling Intelligencer* now called "The Linsley Institute" was that the original school building had deteriorated to a point past repair. In 1854 the old school was torn down and the students temporarily removed to more commodious rooms in the Hardeman Building on the corner of Market and Sixth Streets. The school would conduct its business there until construction of a substantial new facility on present-day Eoff and Fifteenth Streets could be completed. Noah Linsly's remains, which had been buried on the grounds of the original campus, were duly disinterred and rededicated beneath a new monument in Mount Wood Cemetery.

By 1850 Wheeling's population had grown to more than 13,000, including a significant infusion of German immigrants fleeing the dislocations in Europe following the Revolution of 1848. The region's commercial accessibility via the river, the National Road, a suspension bridge spanning the Ohio River (1849), and a newly completed extension of the Baltimore and Ohio Railroad (1853) combined to align the western counties of Virginia with the nation's rising commercial interests, rather than the agrarian slave-supported interests to the south and east. These economic differences, combined with the staunch antislavery convictions of the German immigrants, would propel the western counties to full-blown secession from Virginia by the time Civil War commenced in 1861.

Under the Rev. John Scott's enlightened leadership (1847–52)—he would go on to become president of Washington & Jefferson College—the Linsly Institute continued to attract enough boys, and fewer and fewer girls, to remain in operation. By decade's end, however, it was clear to the school's trustees that the most viable path ahead lay in becoming an all-boys institution, in effect an independent scholastic partner to the now well-established Mount de Chantal. The trustees formally reconstituted the school as all-male in 1861.

The Institute's new building was completed in time for the start of the fall term in 1859. The handsome three-story brick building in the federal style was for decades regarded as the crowning architectural jewel of the city. The teachers and boys would only enjoy their new facility for four years, however, before being temporarily displaced by the newly composed state legislature who converted the instructional spaces into West Virginia's first statehouse. Until they

1 First State House of West Virginia, circa 1861

regained occupancy in 1870, Linsly boys carried out their lessons first in the Odd Fellows Hall on the corner of Twelfth and Chapline Streets, and later in the nearby Fruit Building.

Wheeling in this period of political ferment seemed a logical candidate to become the capital of the emerging new state, despite its location on the westernmost margin of the panhandle. The two Wheeling Conventions assembled in the spring and summer of 1861 formally repudiated the state of Virginia's secession from the union and established the new state of West Virginia, measures readily accepted by President Lincoln. Throughout the war and for two decades after, state legislators would disagree as to the best location for the capital. In what historians have called the "floating capital" period, the seat of government was moved to Charleston in 1870, then formally restored to Wheeling in 1875, only to be removed again, this time permanently, to Charleston in 1885.

Eager and willing to take their abolitionist, pro-Union convictions to battle, the German and other like-minded men of Wheeling organized and outfitted the First West Virginia Artillery to oppose Confederate forces. And while there would not be a specifically military program at the Linsly Institute for more than a decade, older boys in the school were being readied for military service, and the germ of a new mission for the school was conceived.

In the first decade of reconstruction after the war, Wheeling families experienced a number of dislocations and hardships. The decline of silver as a standard for international currency, the sudden collapse of what had been a boom in railroad construction, and devastating drains on national capital caused by natural disasters such as the 1871 Chicago and 1872 Boston fires combined to create the young republic's most severe economic depression to date: the Panic of 1873. Exacerbated by a deadly outbreak of equine influenza, the Panic erupted in bank runs, bank failures, and confrontational labor strikes.

With the city of Wheeling economically stalled, the Linsly Institute stood poised to collapse. Its facility, now fifteen years old, required repairs for which preoccupied trustees were unable to provide the funds. Foreshadowing what would become an inspiring pattern in Linsly's history, a visionary leader emerged who would reshape and reenergize the school—to the extent that excellence, and not mere viability, would define its operation into the coming century.

John Michael Birch (1854–1911) was a pivotal figure in the life of the Linsly Institute and a much beloved figure in Wheeling's civic life. Reared in Claysville, Pennsylvania, near Pittsburgh, he graduated from Washington & Jefferson College and at age twenty accepted the Linsly trustees' invitation to lead the school in the newly designated position of "headmaster." Taking on the struggling school in the heart of a city gripped by a crippling economic depression, Birch recognized the necessity of establishing a clear, distinctive mission and then set about to realize it. Birch served three separate terms as Linsly's headmaster, his service interrupted first by a call in 1881 to be superintendent of Wheeling's expanding public school system. He returned to Linsly in 1889 but was commissioned a year later to serve as Consul to the U.S. embassy in Nagasaki, Japan. Birch returned to Linsly in 1910 and died at his post the following year.

The changes Birch initiated at the school were profound and lasting. The boys' earlier interest in military matters stimulated by the coming war had not abated. Moreover, the fledgling state would be well served by a school preparing boys for military service and command. By 1877 Birch had established a uniformed Cadet Battalion that had its first formal dress inspection and parade on Washington's birthday and staged a "sham battle" the following May. The new military program at the school was at first optional but would grow increasingly central to the school's ethos. By the late 1880s participation in the military program was required, and in 1890 the U.S. War Department recognized the status of the military program, providing the school with both an armory and Springfield rifles for the cadets.

2 John Michael Birch, circa 1885, Headmaster 1874–1911

Birch's vision for the school went beyond adding a military dimension. Immediately on gaining his appointment, he set out to create a rigorous and stimulating scholastic program. Since its founding as a Lancastrian Academy, the school had enrolled children whose parents felt they were school-ready and retained them until they were determined to have achieved basic literacy and practical computational skills. Birch revised the school's prospectus to include, in addition to foundational language and arithmetic training, Latin and Greek, ancient and modern history, German, French, natural philosophy (physics), logic, biology, zoology, as well as a number of applied sciences, including telegraphy, astronomy, and surveying. Within a decade the Institute was enjoying record enrollments of over 100 boys in grades five through twelve, the senior boys prepared to attend premier colleges and universities. By the end of Birch's tenure, the reputation of the Linsly Institute was such that graduates could attend colleges without having to take their standard entrance exams.

Birch understood that scholastic rigor and a habit of intellectual inquiry could not be achieved merely by imposing demanding requirements. He saw academic achievement as a natural consequence, but not the sole aim, of an intellectually stimulating school community. Immediately upon assuming the Institute's headmastership, Birch reached out to neighboring Mount de Chantal to propose joint activities, such as the Linsly Literary Society, established to promote "the improvement of its members, in declamations, discussions, original essays, orations and debates." Through the early 1880s the boys of Linsly and the girls of Mount de Chantal published a decorous bulletin called *The Echo,* consisting of

The Linsly Institute: A New Mission

3 The Oldest Picture of Linsly, circa 1877

verse, short stories, snippets of polite humor, reflections on current school events, as well as essays on such weighty existential matters as "sublimity," "ingratitude," "enjoyment," and "the choice of a profession." The rather arch tone of *The Echo* suggests a student body far from frivolous. A prescient 1881 article titled "Cigarettes" concludes: "Prodigious fortunes have been made and are making, and millions of people are slowly ruining their digestive organs the fouls stuff wrapped up in the various brands claimed to be pure. Let any smoker of cigarettes subject his tongue and throat to a medical examination after smoking a package of cigarettes. Vitriol itself leaves no more sinister impressions on tongue throat and palate." Birch took care to invite the Wheeling public to the Literary Society's Friday afternoon programs.

The new sense of purpose and vitality Birch managed to infuse into the school was inseparable from his concern that the boys in his charge learn civility and decency, an aim well served by the military emphasis on personal responsibility, respect, and deference to rank, loyalty, and bravery. A convinced Christian himself, Birch sought no denominational affiliation for the school but saw to it that a chapter of the Bible was read at each day's drill formation.

By the late 1870s the Linsly Institute's light was clearly out from under a bushel, as Wheeling rebounded from the economic setbacks of the 1873 Panic. The population swelled to 35,000, as horse-drawn public streetcars now plied the city streets. In 1879 the first telephone was installed. The electrification of the city commenced in 1882 when the A.J. Sweeney Company introduced electric lighting to businesses and residences. By 1888 the trolley system would be converted to electric power. Local businesses and banks enjoyed a resurgence, but none more than the Marsh Wheeling tobacco company, a family business founded modestly in 1840 on the premises of the family residence of Mifflin M. Marsh.

The company's highly favored "Marsh Wheeling Stogies" were soon in high demand in the region and then nationally, necessitating new factories first on Water Street then, in 1908, on its historic site on Market Street. Through the remaining decades of the nineteenth century through the middle of the twentieth, Marsh Wheeling Stogies—and their distinctive wooden boxes—were an iconic fixture in American popular culture. A nostalgic nod to their heyday can be seen in the 1999 film, based on Stephen King's prison novel, *The Green Mile:* a prisoner keeps his pet mouse, Mr. Jangles, in a lovingly preserved Marsh Wheeling Stogies cigar box.

4 Linsly Cadets, circa 1890

Birch was called away from the Institute twice to meet public needs. As superintendent of Wheeling's public schools (1882–88), he laid the groundwork for the city's first public high school and established a new and lasting graded curriculum for the earlier grades. As Consul to the Empire of Japan, he was decorated for a series of delicate and successful negotiations with the Portuguese involving their interests in the Pacific. But in the hearts and minds of the people of Wheeling, Birch's crowning achievement was his service to Linsly. Upon his death in 1911, a remembrance published in the *Wheeling High School Record*, the yearbook of the high school he had helped to conceive, observed that Birch's name would be "imperishably connected with the Linsly Institute":

> The impress that Professor Birch made upon the students of the Linsly Institute [consisted in] developing, guiding, and training boys for a useful life in Christian citizenship.

3 | The Great War and a Determination to Serve

In November 1914 the cadets of the Linsly Institute paraded in full uniform to St. Luke's Church on Wheeling Island to commemorate the centennial of the school's chartered founding. The sermon delivered for the occasion, "The Righteous Shall Be Held in Everlasting Remembrance," was delivered by the Rev. Jacob Brittingham to honor the vision of Noah Linsly. Decorous as the occasion was, the school's vital signs were worrying. The enthusiasm for all things martial sparked by the Spanish-American War (1897–98) had quieted nationally, and a sharp economic recession in the first decade of the new century once again threatened the institute's viability.

The healthy enrollments of over a hundred boys that followed Birch's invigorating reforms dwindled after the turn of the century to the point that, by 1906, the year the recession began making its impact, the school struggled to enroll sixty students and would graduate only nine. In the spring of 1907 Linsly trustees entertained a proposal from the Wheeling public schools to merge the institute into a newly conceived public high school. The first vote on the proposed measure was split four votes to four. A month later the board voted again on the proposal and this time decisively rejected it, a change of heart Robert Schramm in his 2003 pictorial history felt may have been inspired by Noah Linsly's original motto "Forward and no Retreat."

Nonetheless, the school's prospects were dire as already unsustainable enrollments continued to decline. In the spring of 1910, trustee minutes solemnly transcribed Headmaster Harry Odgers' assessment of the state of the institute: "Professor Odgers presented his report of the progress of the school in the past year He was not satisfied, and reported that he knew of only 15 boys to enter next fall. He tendered his resignation." With an understandable sense of urgency, the trustees invited a succession of educators to Wheeling to consider leading the foundering school, but all declined. Providentially the board was able to persuade the much beloved John Birch to return to Linsly and attempt to right its course.

5 Linsly's 100th Anniversary Celebration, circa 1914

The decision to remain an independent school did not in itself brighten the Institute's immediate prospects. In addition to the enrollment drain caused by the new public high school alternative and the slumped economy, the once impressive school building at Eoff and Fifteenth Streets was in need of serious maintenance. Birch's return succeeded in lifting the school's spirits, however, and though he would die at his post the following year, the trustees had been sufficiently energized to raise funds to shore up the building and to outfit new laboratories in the sciences. By mid-February 1911, an editorialist in the *Linsly Magazine* could report a school on the rebound:

> . . . The building is a little aged, but the equipment inside is modern and the instructors have modern ideas. The appearance of the building from the outside is deceiving. Strangers enter expecting to find old, worn out equipment and badly arranged classrooms but are surprised.
>
> Then again the military feature is once more to become a fixture at Linsly. This was done away with when the school enrollment dwindled to a small size, but Prof. Birch thinks that it should be reestablished, and so do all the boys now attending. Next fall when Linsly opens it will be once more as a military academy.
>
> Linsly . . . is not quite as large a school as it used to be . . . but it is every bit as good a school and unless the writer is badly mistaken in his deductions it will be but a few years until the old Institute as it did in the days gone by and from all standpoints will be the leading preparatory school in the state.

> Twenty-five students comprise the enrollment at Linsly to-day, and these students are real boys. They are all earnest workers but still they are real boys and are just the sort that form the nucleus of a good school for young men. They are not "molly coddles" or "sissies," but are boys who will study and still have a good time, and there is not one of them that Prof. Birch, the principal, does not want in the school.
>
> Sixteen of the twenty-five entered the school for the first time last September, but those sixteen, under the tutorship of the nine old boys who returned, have acquired the famous Linsly spirit and are now as earnest in their desire for a bigger and better school as those who attended and graduated during the days when the student body numbered far above the hundred mark.

With these improvements, enrollments began to climb again under the leadership of new Headmaster Charles H. Patterson (1913–16), who came to Linsly from West Virginia University where he had for thirteen years been a professor of literature. With increased stability and brighter prospects, the school's academic rigor was restored. The student body was arranged into five successive classes, beginning with a "preparatory class," roughly equivalent to a current eighth grade, followed by fourth year (freshman), third year (sophomore), second year (junior), and first year (senior) classes. Twelve and thirteen-year-old boys were admitted into the preparatory class when they were able to demonstrate competence in arithmetic, including fractions and percentages, a "fairly good" knowledge of geography, some mastery of grammar, and the elements of composition.

Once admitted, the preparatory class would study advanced arithmetic, English grammar and literature, introductory Latin, English history, and penmanship. Fourth class boys would continue into algebra, Latin, English composition and the reading of selected English "classics," classical history (Greece and Rome), and drawing. The third class would take on plane geometry, English rhetoric, Latin (Caesar's *Gallic Wars*), medieval and modern history, an elective course in either German or French, and drawing. Second class boys advanced to solid geometry and advanced algebra, American literature, Latin (Cicero's *Orations*), French or German, chemistry, and drawing. The first class took on trigonometry, advanced English composition and literature (essays), Latin (Virgil), German or French, civil government, physics, and drawing. Greek was also offered to boys in the first class who demonstrated special promise in languages. While the curricular sequence was set for boys intending to apply to college, there was some variation in emphasis depending on whether graduates intended to enter what many colleges and universities designated as "classical" or "scientific" programs. Requirements could also be adjusted for boys who did not intend to continue their schooling beyond the secondary level.

As the school worked to reestablish itself in the city, Headmaster Patterson and his colleagues took pains to articulate the specific educational need that a school like Linsly was uniquely designed to meet. Under the heading "Certain

Advantages of a Private School for Boys," the centennial year catalog for 1913–14 stressed the depth of personal attention Linsly was able to provide: "[It is] of course the special business of the private school to give a carefulness of personal supervision, understanding and sympathy to each boy," adding that "the private school cannot be charged with snobbery. It has in its ranks the poor and the rich and no association could be closer or bring more respect for the man himself, regardless of his financial condition."

The school's centennial reemergence was due in part to a growing economic optimism in Wheeling in the years leading up to World War I. The Fostoria Glass Company was prospering—and hiring—in neighboring Moundsville. On Sunday, April 30, 1911, Pittsburgh's *Gazette Times* broke the news that Wheeling's Mold and Foundry company had been awarded the federal contract to fashion the lock gates for the Panama Canal, construction of which had been underway since 1881 and was due to be completed in 1914.

Though President Woodrow Wilson had won his second presidential term largely on the strength of the slogan, "He kept us out of war," the mounting national interest in the escalating crisis in Europe stimulated a revival of military training in schools of all kinds across the country. Largely for financial reasons Linsly had suspended its military training program in 1910—over the strong objections of many alumni. As it happened, this affront to the sensibility of the alumni cadets gave rise to a crucial boost to Linsly's fortunes. Determined to get the alma mater back on track, the alumni formally organized in 1910 and, in addition to producing its first alumni publication, the *Linsly Magazine*, succeeded in raising funds for needed school repairs and, with war looming, the resurgence of the military training program. In the course of their April 1913 meeting, the trustees unanimously approved the addition to the board of an alumnus trustee selected by the alumni association, thus confirming the role Linsly graduates continue to play in the stewardship of the school.

With the reinstatement of its military program and vigorous new support from alumni, the school's enrollment began to grow. Despite the departing Headmaster Odgers' gloomy 1910 forecast that only fifteen boys were likely to show up for the 1910–11 school year, Headmaster Patterson reported an enrollment of forty boys—thirty of them full-pay—for 1913–14, with the prospect of an additional ten for the coming year. The school in fact would enroll eighty-six boys in 1914–15, causing trustees to record in their minutes that "[Patterson] assumed the position at a time when the prospects for the school were extremely dubious, and by his energy, industry, and inspiration put the school on a firmer basis." In recognition of that energy, industry, and inspiration, the board more than doubled Patterson's salary to $4,000 (the equivalent of approximately $200,000 today)—of which Patterson agreed to dedicate $1,000 to the operating expenses of the school.

In addition to shoring up its scholastic and military training programs, Patterson and his colleagues determined that one of the school's central features—its all-boys composition—needed to be clarified and affirmed. The

The Great War and a Determination to Serve

1916 *Linsly Institute Catalog*, a document pitched to families considering enrolling in the school, included for the first time a section titled "Linsly is not Coeducational":

> It has been established in practice that few girls are interested in mathematics and science, but more girls than boys are . . . found in the language and history classes. Under coeducation the tendency is to emphasize this difference; boys avoid the so-called culture studies, girls the so-called practical ones. On the whole girls surpass boys in subjects where memory and imagination count for most; boys surpass where originality and powers of calculation are demanded.

The catalog went on to propose that boys enrolled in the female-dominated "culture studies" come to "feel it is hopeless to compete with the girls for grades." In single-sex classes, by contrast, those classes are not avoided and effort is not withheld due to the superiority boys perceive in the other gender. Thus, the *Catalog* concluded, in all-boys classes boys' natural competitiveness becomes "both possible and fair."

The trustees' vote of confidence notwithstanding, Patterson departed Linsly in the spring of 1916 to assume a professorship in literature and drama at Massachusetts Agricultural College (now the University of Massachusetts), an appointment he would hold until his death in 1933. Unable to find a gray eminence to fill the headmastership, the trustees appointed two young faculty members, Guy. E. Holden and H. W. Standerwich, to serve as co-principals. Holden, a graduate of Washington & Jefferson, had come to Linsly after teaching and coaching football at Wheeling High School. His extraverted good nature and drive quickly won the respect of the Linsly boys who were duly bereft when Holden was enlisted in 1918 to serve in the European war.

The nation now at arms, it is not surprising that the cadets of the Linsly Institute were fiercely partisan. An editorial in the April 1918 issue of the *Linsly Bulletin,* titled "Deutschland Über Alles," expressed outrage at recent German propaganda maintaining that Prussians were not only the sole race fit to rule the world but that God Himself was Prussian. Infantryman Joe Emblen, a recent graduate now stationed at Camp Logan, Texas, where he was training with the 131st

6 Linsly Cadet Battalion, circa 1916

U.S. Infantry, provided a more personal perspective in an open letter to his former classmates:

> We all expect to see France by the first of January, and I hope we do—any place to get out of Texas. I do believe this state is the hottest state in the union, and has more wild and poisonous creatures than you ever saw. There are thousands of scorpions and rattlesnakes down here. A scorpion's sting is very poisonous this time of year.
>
> . . .We are sure getting enough drilling. We go out in the morning at 7:30 and come in at 11:30; eat our dinners and go out again at 1 p.m. and drill until 5. . .
>
> Boys . . . I sure would like to get a few letters from some of you. Tell me all about the football team and Old Linsly. I still have the Linsly spirit with me; if I did not I could not stand this life at all. . .

The 1918 *Linsly Institute Catalog* announced the military leave of absence of its young principal with special warmth: "Coach Holden has been a prominent factor in the success of the Institute. He is now in training at the Officers Training Camp, Fort Monroe, Virginia. His policies in mathematics and athletics will be continued and strictly maintained. All Linsly is proud of Mr. Holden and will watch with keen interest his work in the service."

More than a hundred Linsly graduates, teachers, and senior students would serve in the Great War. The first of them, cited previously, was seventeen-year-old cadet Joseph Emblen who in 1917 was called up to the Illinois National Guard to prepare for duties abroad. Emblen and his fellow cadets had already been exposed to infantry close-order drills as well as simulated combat lacking, according to the 1917 *Linsly Bulletin*, "only trenches and bursting shells." Four Linsly boys perished in the course of the war. Harry Cooper and Frederick Woods fell in France; Raphael Fawcett (1906) and Earl Chambers (1914) succumbed to the Spanish influenza epidemic before they were posted overseas.

When Lieutenant Holden returned to Linsly as sole principal in 1919, he was greeted by a spirited and fully enrolled school of 103 boys. The March 1919 issue of the *Linsly Bulletin* recorded that when he first addressed the assembled school, "Mr. Holden was greeted from all sides by much applause and cheering." The postwar years, however, posed economic and other challenges that would not be met by maintaining the school as it was.

4 | A Greater Linsly

Despite considerable renovations financed by dedicated alumni, the school building at Eoff and Fifteenth Streets was showing its sixty years. Crowded now with more than a hundred boys attending, the facility was also in need of structural repairs. On the evidence of postwar *Linsly Bulletins,* the cadets mostly took it in good humor that in heavy rains the roof leaked. Aware that the school's central downtown location was better suited for commercial than scholastic use, the trustees began casting about for a potential buyer from the business community. As the school progressed into the 1920s, the need for a new campus, preferably a mile or two from downtown, had become clear.

When Principal Holden resumed his duties in 1919, postwar inflation was straining the school's capacity to meet its fixed commitments. Operating annually at a deficit of about 14 percent of its annual budget, by 1924 the school's total indebtedness had reached $33,000, a present-day equivalent of more than $450,000. By the time the 1923–24 school year commenced, trustees and dedicated alumni had resolved to create nothing less than what the *Linsly Bulletin* would herald as a "Greater Linsly": a gathering of resources from all constituents and throughout the region to build a new campus at a location yet to be specified. The Greater Linsly campaign was given a remarkable kick-start when the Alumni Association put together a complicated lottery in which participants could purchase any number of tickets to Linsly's football games—all school teams were strong that year, especially its record-setting state championship basketball team. Alumni, parents, and students were enjoined to sell tickets, and tens of thousands were sold, purchasers motivated by the staggering grand prize—$15,000.

Through the spring and early summer of 1924 the Ways and Means Committee of the board of trustees, chaired by E. W. Stifel, weighed the school's present resources and the community's capacity to create "A Greater Linsly." The school's assets were computed to be the building and its facilities, valued at $85,000, plus $15,000 in invested endowment, less accumulated debt service of $33,000. Board Chairman H. C. Ogden announced the trustees' resolve to launch a Linsly

Second Century Fund Drive to raise an additional $400,000 for the new facility. Wheeling businessman Louis Bertschy's offer to purchase the old school building for $75,000 was reviewed and accepted, and after considering a number of alternate sites in the city, the board purchased for $12,000 a partly wooded ten-acre site in suburban Woodsdale. The property had been called Thedah Place—*Thedah* being an acronym for the names of the five families (Thalman, Hubbard, Ewing, Dalzell, and Holloway) who had originally purchased the property in order to create a pastoral buffer between their homes and any future industrial development. The trustees determined that the new greener, more spacious campus—a fifteen-minute streetcar ride from downtown Wheeling, ten by automobile—would still be easily accessible to Linsly families.

As anticipated, the Second Century Drive required the dedicated efforts of all Linsly constituents. By the autumn of 1924, Board President Ogden could report that more than half of the campaign's goal, $252,000, had already been given or pledged, enough to proceed with site selection and construction. Teams of students led by faculty captains set out to raise $25,000 for "The New Linsly," and exceeded their goal by $2,000.

The new school would be designed by Wheeling's leading architect—and Linsly graduate—Charles W. Bates (1879–1928). Bates left Wheeling to study architecture and engineering at the Armour Institute of Technology and the Art Institute of Chicago, an experience that would prove to be formative for both Linsly and for Wheeling. Decades earlier Chicago had rebounded mightily from its devastating fire and in hosting the 1893 Columbian Exposition created an expanse of monumental buildings along its lakefront that would inspire a neoclassical building revival throughout the country, the so-called City Beautiful Movement. Bates carried the City Beautiful spirit back to his hometown in his designs for a series of distinctive buildings, including the Capitol Theatre, Ohio Valley General Hospital, Fort Henry Club, Ohio County Public Library, Wheeling Clinic, Stifel Fine Arts Center, and Central Union Building. As both an alumnus of the school and a Woodsdale neighbor of the proposed site, Bates brought an understandable depth of feeling to the design of the stately schoolhouse he presented to the trustees. Two years after the completion of Old Main, Bates' son and namesake, Charles W. Bates, Jr. (1934), was enrolled in the Institute.

Wheeling's leading construction company, R. R. Kitchen, was awarded the contract for the new Thedah Place facility. Ralph Ross Kitchen's firm had established preeminence in the city and in the region, having completed a series of handsome dormitories at West Virginia University, Triadelphia High School, as well as Wheeling's leading banks, stores, and theaters. Construction of the new facility commenced in February 1925 and proceeded with remarkable speed. On May 10, the cornerstone was set in place, and the new Linsly Institute opened its doors to ninety-three bedazzled cadets the following September.

7 Old Main, circa 1952

The new building, which would come to be affectionately known as Old Main, provided a stimulating boost both to the Institute's morale and to its program. The facility, "modern in every respect," according to the 1925–26 *Linsly Catalog,* was a pleasingly balanced neoclassical brick structure of three stories, defined in front by a striking set of columns on each side of the main entrance supporting at roof level an architrave and tympanum. The ground floor housed a gymnasium—"the finest in the Pan Handle," in the estimation of the *Bulletin*—locker rooms, a dining hall, and a boiler room. A double set of stone steps led up to the second, or main, floor housing the headmaster's office, reception room, library, and classrooms. On the third floor were the laboratories, science classrooms, and a spacious study hall. Perhaps no feature of the new campus was more warmly appreciated by the cadets than what the *Bulletin* editors determined were superior playing fields, crowned by "one of the finest football fields in the tri-state area."

The impressive new campus was further graced in 1925 by an extraordinary gift of sculpture, which in the hearts and minds of Linsly students has since come to symbolize the spirit of the school. *The Aviator* was fashioned by one of America's most accomplished monumental sculptors, Augustus Lukeman, the creator of the colossal Confederate Memorial on Stone Mountain, Tennessee. The Linsly statue was the somewhat unexpected gift of Sallie Maxwell Bennett, matron of one of West Virginia's leading political families. The statue represents a winged and uniformed image of her late son, Louis Bennett, Jr., who while flying an allied mission over France in 1918 was shot down by German antiaircraft fire and perished of his wounds. Louis Bennett, raised in Weston, West Virginia, attended boarding schools out of state and then Yale before returning home and attempting to organize a military flying corps that might aid the allied war effort. The federal government, skeptical of the contribution airplanes might make to the war effort—aviation had then existed for barely a decade—ultimately declined to enlist such a unit, so Bennett went to Toronto where he enlisted in the British Flying Corps and was eventually deployed to England. *The Aviator* is one of seven sculptural memorials commissioned by Mrs. Bennett in the United States, England, and France honoring her son and his Royal Flying Force comrades. Inscribed into the plinth supporting the statue is a dedication to Bennett's fallen compatriots, headed by the slogan "Ready to Serve."

8   *The Aviator,* circa 1961

Both the science and the romance of early aviation appealed to the cadets and aspiring engineers of the Greater Linsly. Their enthusiasm was inflamed mightily in the summer of 1927 when the city of Wheeling was able to negotiate a celebratory visit from the most famous flier and most famous airplane in the world. The previous May, Charles Lindbergh's epic 3,600-mile flight from New York to Paris in a specially outfitted monoplane, the *Spirit of St. Louis,* had launched him to instant international celebrity. In the months following it was determined that he would make a flying goodwill tour of the United States, stopping at various new airstrips lining what developers hoped would be a coast-to-coast "Model Airway." Moundsville's Langin Field was the Model Airway's fueling link between Dayton, Ohio, and Washington. Lindbergh was scheduled to land the *Spirit of St. Louis* at Langin on August 4. From there he would be paraded through a continuous throng of well-wishers to an enlarged grandstand in the State Fair Grounds on Wheeling Island where he, Governor Howard Gore, and other dignitaries would address those assembled. On the awaited day the *Wheeling Intelligencer* estimated that 10,000 people were on hand at Langin Field to cheer as Lindbergh executed a perfect three-point landing. In the course of the festivities to follow, more than 100,000 turned out to catch a glimpse of the great man. Immediately upon completing his address to the crowd at the State Fair Grounds, Lindbergh was motored to the Linsly campus where he was greeted by Guy Holden, an honor guard of twenty cadets, and a delegation of trustees. While in Europe, Lindbergh had made it a point to visit memorial sites and lay wreaths of tribute to the past war's fallen soldiers and fliers. At Linsly, with few words and little fanfare, he placed a wreath at the foot of *The Aviator.*

From the new campus's conception years earlier, the trustees had calculated that the Greater Linsly would very likely attract a larger student body. The new building was built to accommodate as many as 250 students—more than twice the enrollments of the postwar years. Principal Holden warned prospective families in 1925 that they had better secure their places early because the next year's enrollment would be "capped" at 250. This may have been more wishful thinking than practical advice, although the school would grow substantially in the years leading to the Great Depression.

9 Charles Lindbergh at Linsly, circa 1927

Dr. George C. Mechlenberg led the capital drive to build the new campus and for a few years after its completion served as the institute's president, while Holden presided over the high school and grade school programs as dean. Mechlenberg was persuaded by major donors that Linsly's now state-of-the-art laboratories could serve not just the school's junior high and high school students but also secondary school graduates seeking the kinds of technical and engineering skills badly needed in the region. Thus when the Institute opened its doors in the fall of 1925, the first twenty Junior College students commenced their studies in industrial and electrical engineering. *Linsly Catalogs* in the years following pointed out that its junior college offerings represented annual savings of $600 to $800 compared to similar programs elsewhere. In the years spanning the removal of Thedah Place and the outbreak of the Second World War, the junior college, and later college, program of the Institute would wax and wane. At no time were the postsecondary programs intertwined with those of the cadets. Junior college students did not wear uniforms and took no part in the military requirements of the school. Many of their classes were held at night, accommodating those with day jobs. Night courses were also offered on an individual basis apart from the degree program. Overall enrollment was further enhanced by the expansion of the pre–high school preparatory

10 Junior College Engineering Students, circa 1925

program, soon to be renamed the Grade School, which beginning in 1925 was open to boys who had completed the fourth grade.

In its considered efforts to serve more boys, Holden and his colleagues broadened the curriculum to create three pathways to graduation. For those intending to proceed to college study, there was still the scientific program. The former "classical" option was modified to a humanities-based "college-preparatory program." A "general" course of study was designed for boys who did not intend to go on to college. The cadets of 1925 were billed $150 for a year's tuition and an additional $50 for uniforms and incidentals.

The impressive new facility and the sense of renewal created by expanded enrollment could not help but boost school morale. Even with its high school enrollment of fewer than a hundred boys, the Institute managed to field strong football, basketball, baseball, and track teams who more often than not bested opponents in what had become a stable league of regional schools. In addition to the archrival Blue and Gold of Wheeling High School, Linsly competed annually with Moundsville, Magnolia, Sistersville, Martin's Ferry, Central, Bellaire, and Union high schools. Linsly's basketball program continued to be dominant in the area. The team's undefeated 1926–27 season was capped by a second state championship.

11 Linsly's 1927 Championship Basketball Team Posing after Winning the Ohio Valley Athletic Championship for the Second Consecutive Season and the Tri-State Basketball Tournament Title at Waynesburg, Pennsylvania

The infectious lift in school spirit encouraged the trustees in 1926 to allocate funds to purchase instruments and pay a director to create the cadets' first military band.

A Greater Linsly

12 Linsly Classroom, circa 1926

The note struck in the 1916 *Catalog* about the special efficacy of all-boys schooling would bear fruit throughout the 1920s. The 1926–27 *Catalog* listed its program offerings under the bold heading, "Better Education for Boys." By the commencement of the 1927–28 school year, enrollment had jumped to one hundred and sixty-two boys in grades five through twelve, plus twenty junior college students and a number of young men who attended night classes in the engineering program on an ad hoc basis. Within just two years the number of students served had nearly doubled.

With new laboratories and a teaching staff able to span high school–level science and college-level engineering, it is not surprising that Linsly cadets tended to excel in and favor their technical studies. In an address to his fellow graduates, 1929 Valedictorian Andrew Nedved took the measure of what he believed mattered most in a young man's education, concluding that the future belongs to "the technical man":

> The technical man has two jobs to perform. One is the process of putting science into industry. It is through the application of the keen intelligence of the engineer to the day's work that the truck and the tractor are supplanting the horse and the mule; reinforced concrete replacing brick and lumber; high tension lines competing with steam engines and fuel oil with coal; not to mention the automatics of various sorts competing with manual labor. It is through the efforts of the technical man of industry that we have such luxuries as automobiles, radios, and electrical appliances...

While Valedictorian Nedved's assessment of the "technical man's" contribution to the nation's prosperity was demonstrably true, it would prove to be "the brokerage man" who would shape the events of the immediate future.

5 | Enduring the Great Depression

When they returned to school in the fall of 1929, Linsly faculty and boys had every reason to expect an especially robust and gratifying school year. Bolstered by a booming regional economy, a record number of students were enrolled: 180 preparatory and high school cadets and 40 junior college students. The trustees reported gifts and pledges to the school's endowment of more than $200,000, most of it dedicated to maintaining the new facility. Nationally, too, a decade of economic growth showed no signs of abating; the stock market was especially strong.

The first sign of trouble ahead was the collapse in September of the London stock market. Not a month later, on "Black Tuesday," October 24, the American stock market followed suit, triggering a complex combination of failed banks, a depressed demand for goods, loss of jobs, and the depletion of corporate and personal holdings. Within a year and a half the entire nation was mired in the most dramatic economic depression in American history. No sectors of the economy were harder hit than agriculture, coal, and steel, and no cities in the region were affected more gravely than Pittsburgh and Wheeling.

The new economic reality brought home to Holden and the school's trustees that despite what had looked like substantial progress in building enrollment and financial support, the school's situation was in fact perilous. The handsome new building cost roughly twice what the old school had cost to operate annually. The trustees had for years balanced annual budgetary shortfalls with compensating gifts from individual donors. Now those donors' funds were depleted if not altogether evaporated. The new 200-plus student enrollment was accompanied in 1929 by a hike in fees to $200 plus $60 for uniforms and incidentals. Now many Linsly families were no longer able to afford it. In consequence, the trustees faced a crisis of trying to meet the school's fixed expenses as the value of their investments collapsed and pledged funds proved to be uncollectible.

By the fall of 1931 the headmaster's report to the board was grim. The operating expenses of the school would exceed available resources by $25,000, equivalent to more than $800,000 in current dollars. The record enrollment of 1929 had dipped by 40 students to 182 in 1930, and 30 more boys withdrew in 1931. The shrinkage of the junior college program was especially disappointing, as the substantial investment in its laboratories and instructors was based on the assumption of healthy enrollment and continuing financial support from industry. During the depth of the Depression the strategy for maintaining the junior college program vacillated from expanding it to a degree-granting three-year Institute of Technology to suspending its operation altogether.

The board duly considered closing the school, or at least suspending its operation, so as to avoid even deeper indebtedness, but Holden proposed another approach. The budget he presented to the board for 1932–33 cut faculty salaries, including his own, in half. With operating expenses thus reduced, the trustees were able to negotiate a second mortgage on the property, enabling the school to stay open, if continuing to accumulate indebtedness. The following year, 1933–34, Holden selflessly proposed that he receive no formal salary at all and that his compensation be determined solely by new revenue he was able to provide by recruiting additional students and from related increases in cafeteria and commissary sales. Throughout the Depression years Holden's life outside of daily school routines was dedicated almost exclusively to urging new families to consider the Institute for their sons and soliciting funds from every financial institution and potential donor in the region. In his pictorial history, *The Linsly School*, Robert Schramm cites Holden's daughter Mary's impression of her father's dedication during these uncertain years: "I remember things were very tough. Every weeknight and many weekends daddy was out beating the pavement, calling on prospective families, trying to get them to enroll... My parents never went to any social functions, daddy was just gone every night." For these efforts Holden would thereafter be justly remembered as "the man who saved Linsly."

Despite the uncertainties created by the new economic reality, for most of the enrolled cadets it was school as usual. The 1931 Valedictorian, Oliver Seitter, acknowledged the challenges ahead in his parting address to his classmates: "What is laid up for us, we cannot know. Hard knocks, we know that. A great deal of disillusion, we know that... We must start at the bottom and work up, we know that." Seitter's remarks were published in *The Cadet*, the new student-produced paper. In addition to reporting general campus developments and sporting results, the 1931 *Cadet* also announced with approval that the annual spring Military Ball would feature dance music from Floyd Mills and his Marylanders, a "hot orchestra" fresh from acclaimed performances at Cornell, Carnegie Tech, and VPI. College matriculation continued to be the ambition of most cadets, and the colleges selected by the class of 1931 were typical of the period: Rensselaer Polytechnic Institute (RPI), John Carroll University (Cleveland), Ohio Wesleyan, University of Pittsburgh, Washington & Jefferson, Carnegie Institute of Technology, Ohio State, University of Pennsylvania, and Linsly's own undergraduate program in engineering.

If anything the ominous outlook of the early Depression years seemed to strengthen the boys' resolve to prevail. As the 1931–32 school year commenced, *The Cadet*, in a spirit of booster-ism, featured the school's song, "The Orange and Black," on the cover of its autumn issue.

Here's to dear old Linsly
We her praises sing
To our Alma Mater
Let every echo ring
True to our colors
We cadets acclaim
Honor, truth, and loyalty
To dear old Linsly's name

Administratively, the Institute continued to be directed by a president who oversaw general operations, including the college program, and a dean who directed both the preparatory grades and the high school. In the spring of 1932 Dr. James Potter succeeded George Mechlenberg as president; Guy Holden continued to serve as dean. The boys at this point were aware of the looming prospect of an unsustainably small enrollment. The June 7 issue of the 1932 *Cadet* ran an appeal headed "Why Your Boy Should Be a Linsly Cadet," stressing the advantages of an all-male faculty, small classes, instruction pitched especially to boys, superior facilities, and day and boarding fees that were a third of those charged at other leading schools. The appeal also noted that Linsly enrolled only "high-type boys," and admitted no one who had not succeeded in his previous school. The 1932 Valedictorian, Christopher Graham, noted the era's special challenges but was confident the Linsly program had prepared him and his fellow cadets to meet them: "…We are in the midst of a peculiar period in the economic history of the world. paralyzed by doubt, insecurity, and suspicion…[but] I think I can say for the class that we shall avail ourselves of this opportunity and in so doing prepare ourselves for the worldly struggle that is to come." Sadly, Graham had only begun to prepare for that struggle when, the following February, he was killed in an automobile accident when he was unable to negotiate a difficult S curve on a rural road outside of Steubenville, Ohio. Newly enrolled at Bethany College, Graham had just learned of his appointment to the United States Naval Academy at Annapolis.

The 1932–33 school year opened on a note of cautious hope. In his opening remarks Dean Holden thanked the boys for helping him over the summer scour the region for 27 new cadets. Including 38 young men in the college division, the Institute now enrolled 162 students, down 45 from peak enrollment in 1929. In the spring of 1933 Old Main was partly flooded by a surging Wheeling Creek following heavy rains. High water partly submerged the ground floor boilers, knocking out the building's heating system. An editorialist for *The Cadet* reported his schoolmates' thundering approval of Dean Holden's "unexpected but not unwelcome" announcement of a four-day vacation while repairs to the boilers were undertaken. Spirits in the assembly hall were heightened further by the elimination of customary morning singing—as some wag or wags had stuffed the grand piano with songbooks, rendering the piano unplayable. Jubilation was dampened somewhat by Holden's subsequent announcement that the lost days would be added to the end of the spring term.

Depression conditions notwithstanding, student life at the institute was enlivened by a number of new cultural initiatives. The thirteen-hundred-seat Virginia Theater on 12th Street in downtown Wheeling had been staging musical, dramatic, and other cultural events since 1908. In the autumn of 1933, within the space of a week, the Linsly cadets were driven downtown to the Virginia for talks by Will Durant, the popular historian of western civilization, and the celebrated aviatrix Amelia Earhart (Putnam). In December they heard writer-adventurer Richard Haliburton describe his travels to Persia, Borneo, and Timbuktu in excerpts from his new best seller, *The Flying Carpet*.

That spring, under the direction of Linsly teacher C. Burl Price, a new dramatic club was formed and proceeded to mount the first in a series of annual musical comedies: *Pickles—or Old Vienna*. With lyrics by Gordon Wilson and Donn Crane, music by Allan Benedict, *Pickles* was one of the first iterations (1925) of a new American theatrical genre, "the high school musical," entertainment written specifically for high school audiences and players. Now popularly felt to be unendurably shallow and kitschy, high school musicals like *Pickles* and *Time Out for Ginger* were much beloved standard fare on school stages through the 1950s. Linsly's 1934 production, featuring dozens of Linsly cadets and young ladies from Mount de Chantal and Tridelphia High School, packed the Virginia Theater for its one-night performance and was duly pronounced a terrific hit by *The Cadet*.

Despite the prevailing isolationist sentiments of the mid Depression years, informed Americans, including some Linsly boys, were alert to the possibility of mounting troubles abroad and the possibility of another, even more catastrophic global war. In his commencement address in June 1934 Valedictorian Robert Strider urged his audience to take heart because "while there be much talk of war and the possibility of a final devastating conflict which may erase the last vestiges of civilization, there is also much talk of peace. . ." Strider would proceed to Harvard University and a career in higher

13 Guy E. Holden, circa 1924, Headmaster 1916–40, "The Man Who Saved Linsly"

education capped by a highly successful presidency of Colby College in Waterville, Maine (1960–79).

Through the mid-l930s Linsly's annual enrollments dipped to worryingly low levels. Holden, whose efforts to recruit new cadets and otherwise keep the Institute financially afloat, was elevated to the Presidency at the outset of the 1935–36 school year. He was succeeded as dean by C. Burl Price. Despite modest enrollments in the 120s, the Cadet Battalion, composed of all the boys in the preparatory and high school program, continued to shine in their annual military inspections, earning for three years running (1935–37) the War Department's highest commendation for arms inspection, platoon, company and extended order drills, formal battalion parade, and performance on classroom examinations.

By 1938 the rise of Nazi Germany and fascist Italy portended another European war, and while American sentiment remained largely isolationist, the cadets of Linsly believed with reason they were likely to be involved. Addressing his graduating class in June 1938, Cadet Captain Lindsey Cowen offered a personal assessment of the ominous developments abroad: "All over the world there is an undercurrent of restlessness, of suspicion, and a perfect willingness to take advantage. What then is the matter with the world? Simply this. Love and cooperation have not been given their proper places. It was ruled out during the World War. It is ruled out now in Germany, Italy, Japan, and Spain..."

Dire developments abroad did little to dampen school spirit. In December 1938 the cadets mounted a festive Founder's Day Dance to commemorate the 125th anniversary of "the oldest school in the Ohio Valley." To accommodate guests invited from area public schools, the dance was held at the Crystal Terrace of the Pythian Building on Chapline Street in downtown Wheeling.

By decade's end there were clear indicators that the worst of the economic depression had passed, although the Institute opened its doors in 1939 to just 108 cadets. Though small in numbers, the student body was plucky enough to continue to field competitive teams against much larger schools in the Ohio Valley. The November 1939 issue of *The Cadet* celebrated its winning football season (6–4), noting "the squad played harder and better than any Linsly team for years." For their efforts the entire team was treated to a trip to Columbus, Ohio, to watch the Ohio State Buckeyes take on the University of Illinois.

Morale was also boosted that fall by Holden's appointment to the faculty of Basil G. Lockhart.

14 Basil G. Lockhart, circa 1940, Headmaster 1940–72

Holden himself was now in failing health, and in what turned out to be his final report to the Linsly trustees, he praised Lockhart, with his newly earned master's degree from West Virginia University, as the strongest appointment to the faculty in the past twenty-five years. The accolade proved to be well founded. Upon Holden's death the following year, the youthful Lockhart assumed the responsibilities as dean, and the following year, 1941, he was appointed "acting" president of the institute. He would go on to lead the school for thirty-three years.

6 | The War Years

Even before the Japanese attack on Pearl Harbor in December 1941, it was clear to Lockhart and his trustees that the coming war would pose new challenges as well as new opportunities. With war looming, the Institute's military training dimension positioned the school favorably in the region. Enrollment through the early 1940s climbed steadily, despite the decline and ultimate loss of the college-level engineering program, as virtually all of the young men enrolled were drafted to fight. Aware of its now positive identity as a military school, the trustees in 1942 took the opportunity to formally amend the school's name to The Linsly Military Institute, thus eliminating the occasional awkwardness of having, for official purposes, to represent the school as The Lancastrian Academy, as it was legally incorporated in 1814.

Both Holden and Lockhart had urged the trustees to consider adding a boarding program to the school as a promising way to enlarge the student body. Boys who lived outside commuting range were occasionally able to enroll if lodgings could be arranged with families in town, but in the absence of an

15 Mr. P. L. Stewart   **16** Mrs. P. L. Stewart

The War Years

on-campus residence Linsly was destined to be a Wheeling day school. That picture changed dramatically when, in 1941, the Merriman family purchased the nineteen-room Thalman mansion in Leatherwood just across Wheeling Creek from Old Main and deeded it to the school. Merriman Hall was quickly readied to house up to forty new boarders for the 1942–43 school year. P. L. Stewart, a warmly regarded mathematics teacher of younger boys as well as a skilled grounds supervisor, and his wife took on *in loco parentis* responsibilities in the new dormitory. In that role the Stewarts became a much beloved fixture in the life of the institute for the next quarter century. Linsly's 1942 *Catalog* assured prospective families that the Stewarts were "a couple of outstanding Christian character whom all boys love and respect. Fortunate indeed are the young men entrusted to their care."

Lockhart's vision for Linsly began to bear fruit even before the boarders arrived. In the fall of 1941 *The Cadet's* banner headline proclaimed "Sixty-four New Cadets Enrolled to Set Record." An encouraging number of the new boys—twenty-five—were entering the freshman class, ensuring substantial and balanced classes in the years to follow. School spirit was also strong that autumn due to some welcome new extracurricular offerings. Lockhart had reestablished wrestling and boxing programs and had augmented the cadets' disciplinary system based on cumulative demerits with merit-based rewards and privileges.

With the rest of the nation, the boys and faculty of Linsly were stunned on December 7, 1941, to hear radio reports that Japanese planes had attacked America's Pacific fleet at Pearl Harbor, sinking four battleships and severely damaging four others. Killed in the raid were 2,402 Americans. As it happened, former Linsly Military Science and Tactics instructor Colonel Peter Salgado was stationed with his family at Pearl Harbor on the day of the attack. Salgado's son Peter, who had been a seventh grader at Linsly before his father's deployment, was also on the island as the bombs fell. His eyewitness account was posted in *The Cadet*.

> On Sunday morning I awakened about 7.30. I began to read the comics. While I was reading I heard a big explosion. (This was a bomb on Wheeler Field.) I thought this was only artillery practice as we have that all the time. In a second this noise was followed by another and then another. We were alarmed. I jumped up to see a plane release a bomb over Wheeler Field.
>
> My dad jumped up and ran out with his helmet, cartridge, belt, and pistol. He assembled the 27th Infantry as he was the Executive Officer of the Regiment.
>
> A little after 8:00 we went outside to see what all the excitement was about. I ran behind bushes and trees when a plane came near. My brother called me a sissy for being afraid. When we were at the end of the street we saw a plane fly right over the barracks spitting fire. We saw the red circle on

the plane. Just then an ambulance scooted by from Wheeler Field. At this we ran home because we were told that it was not a maneuver but a real attack. After a while the plane went away. I went to a friend's house across the street. We listened to news broadcasts. They kept saying "Oahu is under actual attack. Keep off the streets. Keep calm. Stay under cover. The rising sun has been spotted on the wing tips."

Again the planes came. My friend stood out on the street and watched a plane fly over. It was fired on by our anti-aircraft guns from the roofs of the barracks. It flew into a cloud, turned, and dove straight for the barracks, machine-gunning it. My friend jumped and ran for his house.

When the planes had gone for the last time, a guard took us to the barracks as it was more substantial than our frame houses. We ate lunch and supper there. That night we were told we were to be evacuated to Honolulu. After waiting for over two hours in complete darkness and rain, three large buses came. . .

I was piled over with our bags and was not very comfortable. On the way we saw large flashes which may have been big guns. We saw ships in Pearl Harbor burning, also one big fire on land. We saw many tracers flying through the air.

We were sent to different schools, one being called Like Like. Another boy and I slept on a table used for a desk, with one small blanket. Mother stayed up all night with the baby. . .

The United States declared war on Japan the following day, on December 8, and on Germany and its allies three days later. As the nation rushed to mobilize, the Linsly student body joined other Wheeling citizen groups for a defense rally at the Scottish Rite Cathedral where Congressman Robert Ramsay, among other dignitaries, urged the assembled crowd to summon up "the same strength and courage [Americans] displayed in the World War I days of 1918, that they might lead the nation through its present crisis." The resolve of the Linsly cadets was expressed in a February editorial in *The Cadet*.

The United States has been "stabbed in the back" by the hypocritical, power-crazed, puny island of Japan.

. . . Since most of us are too young to bear arms against the enemy, the best we can do for our country is to keep a cool head, go right ahead with our school work. . .and aid directly in building ships, planes and by buying and influencing others to buy [war] bonds and stamps.

The majority of us may see action in the defense of our glorious liberty before the war is over but in the meanwhile let's continue giving all our moral and financial aid to our President and nation and, last but not least, never lose our spirit of victory.

The same issue of *The Cadet* also announced new required classes in military tactics to be conducted by Captain H. D. Haigwood and his colleagues.

The addition of a boarding option combined with the improved wartime economy enabled the Institute to boost enrollment in the fall of 1942 to 169, including another healthy cohort of seventeen new freshmen. Demand for the Linsly program was also sufficient to restore the fifth grade, which had dwindled away during the Depression, to the preparatory program. By December the city of Wheeling had assembled a region-wide Victory Corps to train future soldiers in advance of their enlistment, and Lockhart committed over a hundred Linsly cadets to the effort. When they returned from their winter holiday, the cadets launched a drive to sell war stamps, an effort pitting the five companies of the school battalion against one another for the honor of raising the most funds. According to the February 1943 issue of *The Cadet,* the stamp drive succeeded in raising $1,600 in the first four weeks, with 100 percent participation.

By the spring of 1943, eighty-one Linsly graduates were in active service. Cadet Lieutenant Harry West, valedictorian of the 1943 class, expressed the eagerness that he and his classmates felt to join their comrades in arms. "Fear seems to be an archaic word to the youth of today. Many of us in this class of 1943 have already pledged our minds and our bodies to our country's cause by joining various branches of the service, and we are merely waiting to be called to active duty. . ."

The following autumn, encouraged by the new boarding capability provided by Merriman Hall, the trustees gratefully accepted a gift made by the Weiss family of a second dormitory, the former Dalzell residence in Leatherwood. Robert Dalzell had been a Linsly faculty stalwart in the 1830s. His spacious brick house on Leatherwood Lane had been built to house his eight children and household staff. Its conversion to a dormitory would accommodate nineteen cadets as well as Major and Mrs. Lockhart and their son. The new facility, briefly referred to as Dormitory Two, would soon become Weiss Hall and would house high school–age boys, enabling Merriman Hall under the direction of the Stewarts to lodge the growing number of boys entering the preparatory grades.

The 1943–44 school year was punctuated by the launch of a second inter-battalion competition to sell war bonds. By midwinter *The Cadet* reported that the drive had succeeded in raising $7,500. The holiday season was sweetened considerably by President Lockhart's announcement of the longest winter break in school memory—sixteen days. Throughout the winter and spring of 1944 dispatches from both the European and Pacific theaters indicated cautious optimism that allied victory was not only possible but likely. In May 1944, cadet Valedictorian Joseph Fairi offered his classmates the following advice. "Although victory sometimes seems close at hand, it is wise to face the fact that our enemies are cruel, ruthless and determined to make our road to victory as long and as difficult as possible. Therefore, in order to prepare yourselves for the part that some of you must eventually play in the present conflict, cherish your books and cling to your guns."

With the end of the war now in sight, the school managed to establish a steady trajectory into the Cold War era. Enrollment for 1944–45 was encouraging: 237 students in all, including 54 boarders. The new residential facilities allowed the Institute to position itself as a "national" school, with boys attending from Washington, DC, New York City, Philadelphia, Detroit, and Long Beach, California. Linsly's reputation was such that it continued to attract distinguished visitors. The May 1945 issue of *The Cadet* reported at length a visit to the campus made by Maria Osmena, daughter of the Philippines President Sergio Osmena. Ms. Osmena appeared in the course of a tour to solicit civilian aid in the aftermath of Japanese predations in the islands. *The Cadet* reporter, while expressing suitable humanitarian regard for the visitor's cause, could not resist adding that Ms. Osmena was "young, dark, and darn good looking."

The cadets were in general high spirits as allied victory became a certainty. An editorialist for the May 1945 issue of *The Cadet* urged a respectful moderation in their coming celebrations: "The natural tendency is to celebrate with a lot of riotous living, in drinking, staying out all night, and playing asinine pranks. Let's keep on the straight beam, lock our joy in our hearts and have fun by indulging in some sports or loafing around home or with your next door neighbor..."

7 | Linsly at Mid-Century

Having met the challenges of the Depression and the war years, Major Lockhart and his trustees rededicated themselves to establishing a top-tier college-preparatory school for Wheeling. With annual enrollments of 250 or more and commodious new residential facilities, the Institute continued to position itself as a "national" school, enrolling boys from major cities across the country. Annual costs had risen to $840 for full boarders, $790 for five-day boarders, $290 for high school day students, and $275 for grade school day students. Fees for uniforms and other materials were $100.

In the spring of 1945 Lockhart announced to the assembled school that Linsly had joined the National Honor Society (NHS), an organization established in Pittsburgh in 1921 to recognize scholarship, service, leadership, and character on the part of high-achieving high school students. By 1945 there were thousands of NHS chapters nationwide. Lockhart declared that the Linsly chapter would be named the Guy E. Holden Chapter, a living memorial to "the man who saved Linsly." In a similar spirit of remembrance, a new Memorial Swimming Pool was dedicated in the spring of 1946 to honor the twelve Linsly boys who had fallen in the war: John Sincavich, Robert Fritz, Pearson Jones, Harrison Swalm, Louis Nassif, James Gilleland, Archie McGee, Russell Cracraft, H. W. Brinkman, James Rogers, Marion Nuzum, and Matthew Zabek.

The war now behind them, the Linsly cadets turned their attention to more immediate business, specifically the fortunes of their highly competitive football team, which now played its home games before capacity crowds at Wheeling Island Stadium, obviating the need for the arc lights that had illuminated games played on campus. Ever alert to the possibilities of additional operating revenue, the trustees negotiated a sale of the school's ten stadium lights to Wellsburg High School for $30,000.

In October 1946 Linsly was admitted to the prestigious and then rather exclusive National Association of Independent Schools (NAIS), the first West Virginia school to be so honored. *The Cadet* reported to its readers that inclusion in NAIS marked the Institute as "one of the top preparatory schools in the country." Also in 1946 Lockhart arranged to have Linsly formally accredited by the North Central Association of Colleges and Secondary Schools, an affiliation that would allow the school to benchmark its achievements and standards against other strong schools nationally.

17 Behrens Gym, circa 1948

Boys and faculty alike had good reasons to feel optimistic. Flushed with what *The Cadet* called "overflow enrollment," the boys' spirits were further lifted by the presence of a new dormitory (Weiss Hall), a new pool, a substantial classroom addition to Old Main, and the commencement of construction on a new gymnasium, a gift of the H. Fred Behrens family. Complementing these structural improvements, the cadets as a body distinguished themselves scholastically. Beginning in February 1947 and continuing for a decade, Linsly high school students took a battery of subject-based tests administered by the West Virginia Department of Education, each year averaging 25 percent higher than the average scores of all others tested.

18 Linsly's Only Fourth Grade Class, circa 1945

Linsly at Mid-Century

The increased size of the school enabled an expansion of instructional offerings. Most boys were enrolled in the college preparatory program, but there were also "general" and "technical" pathways to graduation for those who did not intend to proceed immediately to college. The athletic and extracurricular program of the school had also grown steadily through the 1940s. The Institute now fielded competitive teams in football, track, golf, swimming, tennis, wrestling, basketball, and baseball, although the baseball program was suspended from 1947 until 1953 when sufficient numbers enabled the Institute to field competitive teams once again. Boys found intellectual and artistic outlets in the school's glee club, drum and bugle corps, orchestra, school plays, musicals, and annual all-school "minstrels." More cerebral cadets also participated in public debates, oratorical competitions, and essay contests.

The military dimension of the school's program was now long familiar and roundly accepted by the boys and families who chose to enroll. Boys wore regulation military dress at all times when on campus. The flag in front of Old Main was raised each morning and lowered each afternoon by a color guard accompanied by three buglers. The U.S. Army's Fifth Corps formally recognized and periodically inspected Linsly's battalion, typically awarding them top marks for their drills and achievement in their military science classes. Throughout the 1940s and into the 1950s each cadet was trained to fire Springfield '03 rifles.

As cadets proceeded through the high school grades, their rank was upgraded with their demonstrated achievements. Scholastic performance and good conduct were both factors in a cadet's rank. Minor infractions of discipline resulted in "punishment duty," typically after-school marching. Robert Schramm noted in *The Linsly School* that boys chewing gum while in uniform were assigned two hours of marching, as would boys who had misplaced their rifles; failing to salute resulted in one hour of marching, unshined shoes a half-hour. Cadets who exceeded the prescribed maximum punishment duty hours for any thirty-day period were liable to be expelled. Serious offenses, such as intoxication or stealing, invariably resulted in expulsion. Cadets who had achieved noncommissioned or commissioned officer status were held to higher disciplinary standards and stood to be demoted for their lapses. In Schramm's words (he was a 1952 graduate), "It soon became clear to a new cadet that he was at Linsly to work and learn and not to fool around."

From the inception of the military program in 1870 until its dissolution more than a century later in 1979, the martial dimension of school life, though never strident, was a deeply felt part of a Linsly boy's experience. A central tradition through those years was Final

19 Final Drills, circa 1963

Drills, in which each of the companies composing the Institute's battalion competed for top honors in performing elaborate close-order marching drills they had practiced throughout the year. Conducted on the manicured grounds of Wheeling Island Stadium before Linsly families and other guests, Final Drills served to mark the end of each school year, as did the passing on of the ceremonial battalion sword from the graduating Cadet Major to his successor from the rising junior class.

The social highlight of the school year was the Military Ball. Held in mid-May when Wheeling was in full blossom, these formal dances were sometimes preceded by a dinner party ceremonially hosted by the Cadet Major. Upperclassmen attired in parade dress and sabers escorted their female guests in floor-length ball gowns to elegant rooms in, first, the Scottish Rite Cathedral, and then later the Pine Room of Oglebay Park. Each female guest was issued a dance card indicating the schedule of dances to be played by the orchestra—waltz, fox-trot, two-step—and the cadets would negotiate with the young ladies they hoped would consent to a dance.

20 Linsly's Military Ball, circa 1942

Few graduates of the Institute in the Thedah Place era left the school without vivid memories of a school-threatening flood. Aware from the outset that the new campus might be susceptible to flood damage from Wheeling Creek's high waters, the construction of a flood wall was ultimately rejected by the trustees as too costly. In consequence, few years passed without some threatening incursion from the creek. Outright floods in 1943 and 1948 caused extensive damage to the ground floor and first-floor facilities of Old Main. An abiding concern in flood season was whether the footbridge linking Merriman Hall cadets to the main campus on the other side of the creek would hold. The original bridge, designed and constructed in 1942 by a school crew consisting of P. L. Stewart, Henry Brown, and Douglas Haigwood, enabled Merriman Hall residents to avoid what would otherwise have been a two-mile hike or drive to the main campus. Rebuilt and strengthened in 1953 and again in 1963, the footbridge was one of the landmarks of Linsly life through the mid-century.

21 Flood at Old Main, circa 1948

Another highly distinctive feature of Linsly life throughout the mid-century was the annual Minstrel. Minstrel shows, which historians have identified as America's distinctive contribution to musical theater, originated before the Civil War and were highly popular in both the north and south through the turn of the twentieth century. The first minstrel shows were performed by white performers in blackface and included a number of stock characters from the plantation era south as well as a succession of songs, comedy sketches, and dance numbers. Unthinkable today, given the shows' demeaning racist elements, Minstrels were widely performed in all regions of the country through the early decades of the past century before giving way to vaudeville and variety shows.

22 Swinging Bridge after the Flood of 1943

The Linsly Minstrels were the brain child of faculty member Captain Douglas Haigwood, whose many contributions to the school included administration of military discipline, social studies instruction, drill instruction, and direction of choral and orchestral music. When interest in the school's annual operettas showed signs of waning, Haigwood orchestrated the first Linsly Minstrel in 1938, drawing on a majority of the student body as well as girls from Mount de Chantal and other schools. Reliance on stock minstrel characters—a white "interlocutor" (master of ceremonies) and comic "end men" (clownish wise crackers in blackface)—would continue through the 1950s before the shows melded into Extravaganzas, which were in effect elaborately orchestrated all-school variety shows. These all-school entertainments served to identify and celebrate a wide range of students' musical and other talents, and they were highly popular. Given their scale, they required a large auditorium. The first Minstrels were staged in the Madison auditorium on Wheeling Island. In 1945, in order to accommodate citywide interest in the productions, the Minstrels were performed at the Virginia Theater downtown, then, beginning in 1963, at the Capital Theater where Linsly Extravaganzas annually sold out the 2,000-seat auditorium.

23 Captain Douglas Haigwood, Creator of the Linsly Minstrels, circa 1956

That the Extravaganzas were enthusiastically attended by hundreds of people unconnected to the school is a testament to the high production values established by Haigwood and his colleagues. By all accounts the talent on display was considerable. In the late 1980s, for example, the shows were brightened by the singing and guitar playing of a shyly smiling middle schooler, Brad Paisley. Paisley would go on to be a country music superstar, both singer and songwriter, recording a series of gold and platinum records including sixteen *Billboard* number one country hits. In 2008 the Country Music Association named him Vocalist of the Year and in 2010 Entertainer of the Year. In 1988 Paisley chose to finish his schooling at John Marshall High School in order to be closer to his family. In a touching letter to Linsly Headmaster Reno DiOrio he confided, "I shall however miss some of my close friends at Linsly. They and the staff, especially you, make a decision like this very hard... I will always keep Linsly a part of my life and am proud of my achievements there. Forever a friend, Brad Paisley." As a token of that pledged friendship, Paisley returned to Linsly in the course of a 2002 Welcome Home concert in Wheeling to present the school with a framed Platinum (more than a million recordings sold) album, *Who Needs Pictures*, dedicated to the school and presently on display in the Coudon Ogden Library.

At mid-century the Institute had once again become one of the defining institutions in Wheeling. By any measure a strong college preparatory school and the only boys' boarding school in the region, Linsly could boast not only impressive academic achievement school-wide, but a succession of highly successful individuals, young men who attributed their subsequent accomplishments to the standards they were challenged to meet in the course of their school days.

Many notable athletes distinguished themselves in the course of the school's resurgence after the war, but perhaps none more than John Reger (1950). A spirited sports feature in the November 4, 1949, issue of *The Cadet* concluded its review of that autumn's winning football season with, "If there is a boy who deserves the title Football Player of the Valley, it is John Reger." Reger had been a standout contributor to Linsly football throughout his high school career, beginning as a tackle and then emerging as an end and finally as an almost impossible-to-tackle running back. The captain of the nearly undefeated (9–1) 1949 squad, he was recruited to play at Pitt where after less than a year he was a walk-on for the Pittsburgh Steelers as a linebacker. Reger would achieve all-Pro status in the NFL, playing for the Steelers and the Washington Redskins. In the course of his twelve NFL seasons, he was named to three Pro Bowl teams.

24 John Reger, Class of 1950

But strong as its mid-century athletic teams were, the Institute continued to provide a variety of ways in which boys could excel. For example, the feature story cited previously praising John Reger's contribution to Linsly football was composed by the team's student trainer and *The Cadet* sports editor Don Hofreuter (1950) who, among many other distinctions, was named Cadet Major of the Linsly Battalion his senior year. The top scholar and valedictorian of his class, Hofreuter went on to Princeton and then to the College of Physicians and Surgeons at Columbia where he completed his medical training. Specializing in family practice, Hofreuter returned to Wheeling where, in 1968, he was named a Linsly trustee—and the football team's doctor. He was elected chairman of the board in 1975, and through forty-five years of continuous service has guided the school through its most critical transitions, including the termination of the military program and the conversion to coeducation.

25 Cadet Major Don Hofreuter speaking before the class of 1950. Since then, he has served more than forty-five years on Linsly's Board of Trustees

Neither the Institute's unapologetic martial tone nor its athleticism could suppress the musical and artistic impulses of the cadets. In addition to the enthusiastic and widespread participation in mounting the Minstrels and subsequent Extravaganzas, Linsly boys made their presence known in the larger community. In the early 1950s, four musically gifted cadets formed a stirring Dixieland quartet, the Cannonball Four, composed of Robert Schramm (trumpet), Tony Salvatori (trombone), Howard Oliver (drums), and Evan Dadakis (piano). The Cannonball Four were invited to play at a number of prominent Wheeling venues, including the Capitol Theater downtown. The group was also invited to perform a guest spot for the early Pittsburgh TV station WDTV-Channel 3.

By the autumn of the 1950–51 school year enrollment had reached 270, and the school's vital signs were encouraging. Headmaster Lockhart, generally on the lookout for speakers and public figures whose presence might stimulate his colleagues and boys, invited Father Nicholas Wegner, the principal of Boys Town in Omaha, Nebraska, to address the school. Boys Town may at that time have been the most famous school in the United States, due in large part to the dedication of its founder, Father Edward Joseph Flanagan (1886–1948). In 1917 Father Flanagan, then a parish priest in Omaha, founded a school for orphan boys. Boys Town offered a number of distinctive features, including a governing structure in which the resident boys, under the direction of a boy mayor, determined the tone and direction of the school. Launching its graduates successfully into the world for decades, Boys Town and Father Flanagan attracted considerable attention culminating, in an Academy Award–winning film, *Boys Town*, starring Spencer Tracy as Father Flanagan and Mickey Rooney as a plucky resident. In his address to the cadets Father Wegner discussed Boys Town's defining features, including its enrollment of boys age ten to sixteen and the requirement that they each master a "self-sustaining trade."

While Linsly's course offerings included a full range of arts and humanities, the program continued to appeal to what 1929 Valedictorian Andrew Nedved believed would be America's man of the future: the "technical man." The February 9 issue of *The Cadet* noted that, on the basis of Linsly graduates' demonstrated performance there, MIT had announced it would admit any Linsly boy in the top 20 percent of his class without prerequisite exams. Whatever the academic leanings of the cadets at mid-century, it is impressive that the quality of one's mind continued to be an interesting question. In the March 21, 1952, issue of *The Cadet* an editorialist addressed "the qualities of an educated man," concluding with a series of questions: "(1) Do I want to know the truth, or merely verify my own opinions? (2) When I get a new fact, can I put aside my own notions till I find out if this new knowledge can change my view? (3) Can I examine personally why I hold certain ideas?"

By the early 1950s, as enrollments reached and then exceeded 300, the school calendar assumed a familiar rhythm. Rigorous academics, competitive athletics, and military drill were leavened by the fall Senior Play, the Holiday Dance at Christmas, the Minstrel in March, the Hi-Y Dance in April, the Military Ball in May, Final Drills, and Commencement. Graduates attended a considerable range of regional and national colleges and universities. The class of 1954, for example, sent one or more boys to Ohio State University, Dennison University, the Air Force Academy, West Virginia University, University of Cincinnati, Villanova, Bethany College, Washington and Lee, Muskingum, Brown, Duke, Harvard, and Vanderbilt.

By the middle 1950s increased regional interest in the Institute was straining existing facilities. In the fall of 1955 a wing was added to Weiss Hall to accommodate the growing number of boarders. Linsly opened its doors that year to a record enrollment of 306, including the largest senior class, fifty-two, in the school's history. Twenty-five of the new cadets were from Pittsburgh, strengthening what had already been strong ties to that city. Pittsburgh's regard for Linsly was apparently not limited to scholarship. On June 2, 1956, *The Cadet* reported that the then-struggling Pittsburgh Pirates organization—for several running seasons occupying the cellar of the National League—had written to Linsly baseball coach Walter Wilson asking to have a look at "boys who might have a future in baseball." Coach Wilson reportedly sent on the names of seniors Ralph McGraw, Ned Pell, Larry Wells, and sophomore Frank Auth. And while none of the boys recommended would go on to help the Pirates, the team did improve its record to sixty-two wins and ninety-two losses that season, elevating their standing to a tie with the Chicago Cubs for last place in the league.

Linsly at Mid-Century

The later 1950s were marked by an emerging cultural restlessness, much of it generated by the wave of postwar "baby boom" children now entering their teens. Heralding this cultural shift was a new music, rock and roll, and its iconic performers, most notably Elvis Presley. Despite required military dress and clear prescriptions for grooming, the allure of the new teen idol image was not lost on certain Linsly cadets. An editorial in the March 29, 1957, issue of *The Cadet* announced a "crackdown" on "D.T." ("duck tail") haircuts much in vogue beyond the institute's gates. As the editorialist archly explained, "A crew cut in front followed by a long wave in the back looks very unbecoming to a man in uniform." The consequences of showing up for morning drill with a D.T. were unambiguous. The offending cadet would flunk inspection and be sent immediately to a local barber.

Scholastically, Linsly continued to prepare its cadets impressively for their undergraduate programs. Current trustee James McNulty (1960) credits the rigor and personal attention of his teachers in the Lockhart era for preparing him to meet the scholastic demands of West Point. He is especially appreciative of his junior and senior English teacher Gordon Crawford (Linsly 1958–65) for insisting on technically flawless composition, even while opening his eyes to Shakespeare and other classic texts. McNulty also acknowledges the superior instruction he felt he received on the mathematical and scientific side of the curriculum, particularly in Henry Brown's chemistry and advanced math courses. As McNulty recalls, Brown had urged him to apply to his alma mater, Carnegie Tech, and when McNulty chose West Point instead, Brown thereafter refused to speak to him. "But," McNulty adds, "he was a great teacher!" McNulty has since honored the service of his formative teachers by establishing four permanent student scholarships as well as generously supporting the school's capital projects.

Gordon Crawford, who would become the chairman of the English Department, made an indelible impression on many of the boys he taught. Cadet Major Jim Hazlett (1959) recalls that Crawford was brought to the school to shore up

26 James McNulty, Class of 1960

27 Henry C. Brown, Advanced Math and Physics Instructor, circa 1952

what had become "disappointing" verbal SAT scores on the part of Linsly cadets. In addition to correcting this situation dramatically, Crawford, a diminutive Englishman with a pronounced accent, impressed Hazlett and his classmates as an inspired taskmaster. "He was virtually correct in his assessment, both about us as individuals and us in our efforts to glide by without a whole lot of muss or fuss—or bother to read the books, to write the essays, or even to spell the words correctly. Crawford wasn't so much on appearance as he was on demanding flat-out, top-quality performance. He wanted the latter from us and knew that most of us had the former foremost in our thoughts." In addition to shoring up Linsly boys' English composition, Crawford apparently also had the gift for imparting a lasting appreciation of great books. Hazlett remembers fondly Crawford's spirited in-class recitations from George Orwell, Thomas Wolfe, and George Bernard Shaw. He also remembers—with less resentment than wonder—being bent over Crawford's lap and paddled in front of his wildly amused classmates on the final day of classes for the offense of "being a bit of a prig."

The March issue of *The Cadet* also announced the passing of one of the central figures in the second century of the school's life, Dr. Ivan Fawcett. He and his brother, Raphael, both graduated from the Institute in 1906, Raphael as Cadet Major, Ivan as Cadet Captain. Raphael was the first Linsly graduate to die in World War I. Ivan would go onto medical school specializing in ophthalmology. Back in Wheeling he became a civic leader, serving, among many other commitments, as a director and president of the Oglebay Institute. He joined the Linsly board of trustees in 1924 and became its chairman in 1943, serving the school actively until his death. Dr. Fawcett's three sons, York, John, and Alan, were prominent fixtures in the school from 1929 through 1937, as were, a generation later, his grandsons, Ronald, John, Brian, and Timothy, who were enrolled between 1955 and 1975. In all, the Fawcett boys were enrolled at Linsly for a total of seventy-two school years. The Fawcett family has continued to support the school, establishing a Memorial Infirmary in honor of Ivan Fawcett. Subsequent gifts from Alan and Jane Fawcett helped to establish what is now the DiOrio Alumni Hall as well as the present alumni and development offices; in 1999 and 2004 the Fawcetts also endowed two permanent student scholarships. The sense of dedication and continuity represented by the Fawcetts was expressed in a memorial poem published that year in *The Cadet* shortly after Ivan's death. In the poem an aged pilgrim has just completed an arduous, daylong passage over a deep chasm and determines to build a bridge that will make the journey easier for others. Asked why he would make such an effort, the pilgrim responds:

28 Ivan Fawcett Posing for His Fifth Grade Portrait, circa 1898

Linsly at Mid-Century

The pilgrim raised his old gray head
"My friend, in the path that I have come," he said,
"There followeth after me today
A fair haired youth who must pass this way."

As Headmaster Lockhart and his colleagues prepared to launch the 1957–58 school year, he and the board of trustees were informed that plans to extend Interstate 70 through West Virginia would have a direct impact on the Linsly campus. Ultimately, construction of the new highway would require the demolition of both the headmaster's residence and Weiss Hall, which was later removed and rededicated when the school acquired and renovated the McElhinney residence on Leatherwood Lane. The routing of the interstate also required altering the course of Wheeling Creek as it passed through the campus and thus the rebuilding of the school's swinging footbridge. The bridge project was supervised once again by Captain Haigwood, whose initial bridge, constructed in 1942, had withstood every subsequent flood and from whose planks not a single cadet had fallen into the creek in the course of thousands of crossings.

Despite the demands of new construction, the Institute's program and routines continued apace through the end of the decade. The dislocations and cultural strains of the coming 1960s were yet to be experienced at the school. Enrollments climbed steadily into the mid-300s, as Linsly consolidated its reputation as an excellent college preparatory school, unrivaled in the region. So strong was the mathematics acumen of the cadets by decade's end that when the Mathematics Association of America administered a competitive test statewide, not only was the top prize awarded to Linsly senior Andrew Johnson, but second and third prizes went to his fellow cadets senior Gordon Mendelson and sophomore Marc Levenson. As the Institute approached its 150th anniversary, there was much to celebrate.

In preparation for his classmates' fifty-fifth Linsly reunion in the spring of 2014, Mike Murray (1959) summoned up the aura of the school in the late 1950s in a poem.

Forward March, pass through time.
Noah Linsly's learning line.
A living will of true tradition;
And endowment of a man of vision.
A four year taste of erudition.

...Forming years of polished brass,
Freshman plebe to senior class
From fifty-five to fifty-nine.
I had the locker next to Meyn.
Marching along the Linsly Line.

8 | The Challenges of "The Sixties" Era

ON NOVEMBER 1, 1963, *THE CADET* ANNOUNCED IN A BANNER HEADLINE THE school's ambitious program to celebrate its sesquicentennial year, the festivities in May to be directed by trustee Dr. Alan Fawcett. Unbeknownst to most of the boys that autumn, planning was already in progress to transplant the entire campus across Wheeling Creek, a transition to mark nothing less than a new era of Linsly life. In support of the impending festivities the cadets organized a new Pep Club with an aim "to boost attendance at varsity football games and to provide a focal point for cheering and school spirit."

Three weeks later, on November 22, the assassination of President John Fitzgerald Kennedy in the course of a motorcade through Dallas, Texas, dampened more than the Institute's school spirit; it injected a note of confusion and doubt about past verities. In the ensuing cultural climate it would become harder to take for granted the civility and sense of national unity and purpose that had arisen during the peaceful and prosperous postwar years. In this new climate the Institute's foundational premises and values would be tested.

In May 1964, stimulated by what was then the Institute's largest single gift, a million dollar challenge grant from Mrs. Sophie Banes of Philadelphia, the trustees set out

29 Sophie Banes Breaking Ground at the Banes Hall Commencement, circa 1966

to match the sum in order to construct a new "Old Main" across the creek from Thedah Place, the facility designed to accommodate 400 boys. The new schoolhouse, today Banes Hall, would be built on what had been the Pearson estate on Knox Lane at an estimated cost of $1.5 million. Educational consultant Dr. Edwin Crutter was retained to work with architect Woodward Franzheim to match the facility to the school's distinctive program. It would prove to be just one of Woodward ("Woody") Franzheim's generous contributions to Linsly's future. The Byrum Construction Company won the contract to construct the new facility. As in 1925 when architect Charles Bates's original Old Main came to symbolize a Greater Linsly, the prospect of an all new, state-of-the-art schoolhouse promised an invigorating new era in the school's life.

But as ground was broken for Banes Hall in 1966, there were intimations of a more troubled national mood and a changing educational climate. The escalation of the war in Vietnam and an intensified national focus on racial inequality had begun, first in the leading universities on the west and east coasts, then in colleges and schools across the country, to divide the generations—students and faculty, parents and children—on issues ranging from lifestyle to military service. While to a large degree a haven from such discontent, the Linsly community was hardly unaware of the cultural shift. A *Cadet* editorialist in the June 5, 1965, issue opined on "What Gives with Today's Youth," noting:

30 Banes Hall, circa 1970

> We see a teenage boy with his hair combed like a Beatle's. We see another with his trousers so tight we wonder how he gets them on or off. We see a third wear out five dollars worth of tires getting his car underway. The *Daily Globe* tells of a fourth caught stealing. A fifth smokes and drinks beer, maybe whiskey. Another has orange or green hair. . .

The writer concluded that these decidedly non-Linsly youthful types were likely to grow out of it, reassuring readers that these very rebels and delinquents "will one day heal your wounds, fight your legal cases, lend you money or bear your grandchildren. All is not lost. . ."

All was certainly not lost at the Institute. When Banes Hall was opened for business in the fall of 1968, with benefactress Sophie Banes and her two recently graduated grandsons, Richard and Lester Jarboe, in attendance at the celebration, enrollment had climbed to a record 408 boys. But shifting cultural attitudes—including newly strident antimilitary and antidraft sentiments—were inevitably felt by the cadets who went about their daily scholastic business in uniform. In the October 28, 1966, issue of *The Cadet,* editorialist David Keith urged his fellow classmates to "walk tall" in the presence of detractors. "If a cadet is teased about his uniform, he should not try to find a corner to hide in. He should walk taller and show that he is happy to be a Cadet..."

The political leanings among the cadets were decidedly conservative, as might be expected of students and families who had chosen the school for its military program and for the rigor of its traditions. As late as 1968 the all-school variety show was still a "minstrel." In a mock election conducted as the presidential campaigns of Republican Richard Nixon and Democrat George McGovern were drawing to a close, the cadets voted for Nixon by a two-to-one margin. That conservatism notwithstanding, student voices in the closely faculty-monitored *Cadet* began questioning established practices. In the November 8, 1968, issue of *The Cadet* editorialist Ron Sigal challenged the program's emphasis on grade-based motivation versus personal interest and the reward of knowledge for its own sake: "In many cases development in one field is stunted for fear another subject may suffer for it. To someone interested in science, foreign languages may be a bore and a waste of time." The following March an unattributed editorial took aim at the centerpiece of the disciplinary system, Punishment Duty (P.D.). "For years P.D. has existed without any major change. Without improvement it may soon become meaningless. The threat of P.D. has very little persuasion. It is obviously not effective in the prevention of rule-breaking because every day the P.D. line is filled with constant offenders."

By decade's end Linsly students and faculty, as in other independent schools across the country, were struggling to determine what must be maintained and what must be changed in the face of so much cultural tumult, including a widening rift between what children and adults believed should be the extent of the former's freedom and mobility. In the unsettling aftermath of the Kent State University shootings on March 4, 1970, in which rattled National Guard soldiers opened fire on demonstrating students, killing four of them and permanently disabling another, Linsly faculty and boys worked to put the event into perspective—Kent State was a mere two-hour drive from campus. In the May 22 issue of *The Cadet* senior Tom Rownd proposed guidelines for challenging the status quo. "Certainly students should take stands on current issues and policies and should participate in demonstrations if they feel their positions should be voiced. They have the right to demonstrate—only as long as their actions do not disturb the rights of others as at Kent State." Linsly's Assistant Headmaster (Col.) F. C. Houghton, appointed the previous year from Newark Academy, offered a less equivocal view in a special column he had initiated in *The Cadet,* The Colonel's Corner. "If you are really interested in meaningful change and helping to bring it about," Houghton wrote, "avoid the now classic trappings of the political activists.

Beards, beads, and bells are a real obstacle to genuine communication between the groups that must communicate. This new left uniform will get you written off by the people you want to reach..."

Kent State was not the only Vietnam-era event to bear directly on the Linsly community. Linsly graduates, some of them very recent, had served and perished in the war. Air Force Lieutenant Raymond Salzarulo (1960) was shot down in the course of a mission over North Vietnam in 1966. He was believed to have been captured and held as a prisoner of war, but no information about him had been disclosed by his captors. Salzarulo's wife appealed to Headmaster Lockhart for help, and in consequence the Institute's English faculty enjoined their students to begin a letter-writing campaign to North Vietnam President Ton Duc Thang asking for information confirming the life and whereabouts of Captain Salzarulo. The letter-writing campaign bore no immediate results, but in 1973, Lieutenant John Nasmyth, the pilot of the plane in which Salzarulo was the bombardier, was released after six years' incarceration as a POW and returned to the states. He indicated that Salzarulo was killed when the plane was struck. While missing, he was promoted by the Air Force to the rank of Captain. His remains were finally returned to the United States in September 1990.

Entering the new decade, a decided uneasiness had descended upon the student body. Repeated student appeals for more and better school spirit were met with enough resistance and passivity that *The Cadet* editor Benjie Franklin would write this valedictory assessment of his classmates, titled "What You See Is What You Get."

> In several days another senior class will graduate. Some of us will have left an imprint on Linsly either academically or athletically, while others have occupied classroom space, contributing nothing at all to the improvement of the school...
>
> Unfortunately too many seniors at Linsly have wasted their time here trying to shirk responsibilities instead of welcoming them. In the opinion of those people, their days at Linsly have been a waste, which of course they have...

In February of the following year Trustee Chairman Robert Hazlett announced that after thirty-two years of service to Linsly, Colonel Lockhart would resign as headmaster at the end of the school year, to be succeeded by the Upper School dean and teacher of mathematics and sciences (Maj.) Harry Chorpenning. Lockhart's long tenure at the school represented a period of remarkable continuity and growth, bringing to full realization the vision for a new and prosperous Linsly tenaciously husbanded by Guy Holden during the perilous Depression years.

To his colleagues and the cadets Lockhart had become an imposing and occasionally stern personage. As one of his younger colleagues reflected, "There was no question as to who was in charge." Well out of his earshot cadets might refer to Lockhart as the Big Green Lizard, a reference to an outsize green sedan their headmaster favored. Lockhart administered discipline swiftly and firmly. Boys caught fighting were called to his office, issued boxing gloves, and instructed to finish the fight under his supervision—or, if they chose not to, to box Linsly's physically imposing football coach, Jim Hawkins.

From the outset of his headmastership, Lockhart had established himself as a physically commanding disciplinarian. Andy Grimes (1944) recalls Lockhart addressing senior cadets in study hall to announce some new rules. There would be no smoking of any kind, no chewing gum or candy in the corridors or classrooms, and no chewing tobacco. At the mention of the latter, Gigi Easton, a menacingly tough football player seated next to Grimes, spat out a chaw of tobacco into his inkwell, creating a stir in the immediate vicinity. Sensing something amiss, Lockhart made his way to Easton's desk, hoisted him up by his uniform collar, and carried him out into the hallway, the ensuing silence broken only by a younger cadet crying out, "He's going to kill him!"

Mel Kahle (1953) was in the fifth grade when he was summoned one morning to Major Lockhart's office. He had committed an infraction or two before, for which he had been disciplined by Captain Haigwood. But Major Lockhart! Kahle remembers entering his office only to receive the Major's congratulations to his father for having the previous day successfully defended a woman in court who had been accused of murdering an abusive lover. Accepting Lockhart's good wishes with a salute, Kahle recalls being "in shock—and greatly relieved."

Whatever hard edges Linsly cadets may have experienced in the Lockhart era were frequently softened by the caring ministrations of Lucille Munn, one of the institute's longest serving and most beloved staff members. Over nearly fifty years of service to the school her official duties ranged from headmaster's secretary, to bookkeeper, to alumni secretary, but she is best remembered for uncountable kindnesses to boys in need of a sympathetic ear and a word of encouragement in the course of a disappointing day. Before the school's impressive archives were assembled in what is now the school's museum, Miss Munn faithfully compiled volumes of scrapbooks documenting every printed reference to Linsly, its current students, and its graduates. Today Lucille Munn's photograph is framed prominently above the mantelpiece of the Linsly Museum archives room.

31 Lucille Munn, circa 1975

The Challenges of "The Sixties" Era

A tribute composed for the school yearbook, *At Ease,* by Lockhart's teaching colleague Henry Brown characterized the Lockhart era as "An Age of Building" in which the Institute grew from a single schoolhouse and a caretaker's residence in 1940 to a thirty-five-acre campus of thirteen buildings, including a full boarding program. Under Lockhart's stewardship, the school enjoyed balanced annual budgets as enrollments increased steadily from 120 to 360.

For the boys of the school, to whom their headmaster represented the length and shadow of Linsly, Lockhart's departure represented nothing less than the end of an era. A farewell tribute published in the May 24, 1972, issue of *The Cadet* acknowledged their leader's compassionate side.

32 Headmaster Lockhart with a Student, circa 1972

> . . . There was another facet to the Colonel's disciplined make-up. This is the one that has revealed itself in social responsibilities and tenderness, and in sympathy shown in representing Linsly in calls to bereaved parents, in many visits to funeral homes to pay respects for a lost brother or sister. On such occasions the Colonel was at his best, as he was also on numberless trips to hospital rooms to cheer ailing students. Never was the warmth and comfort of this man unequal to the need.

For the duration of his retirement Lockhart would retain his campus residence, dining occasionally with the DiOrios and sharing impressions of campus developments. DiOrio remembers Lockhart as a thoughtful and gracious presence, and in 1981 established the Basil G. Lockhart Award to be conferred on the member of the junior class who will serve the following year as Head Prefect.

However much those attending Lockhart's Final Drills and Commencement in the spring of 1972 might have sensed the end of an era, few could have imagined the challenges and the critical changes that lay in the years directly ahead—changes that would give rise to the next defining period in Linsly's history.

33 Basil G. Lockhart at His Retirement Party, circa 1972

In February 1972, on the brink of his retirement, Colonel Lockhart wrote a letter to John Brisbane, director of admissions at West Virginia University, supporting the candidacy of Linsly senior Stephen Wright for admission to the entering freshman class. Wright, Lockwood noted, "will be the first boy of his race to graduate from this one hundred fifty-eight year old school." It would be more than a decade before a noticeable African American presence was a feature of the school's life.

Quite apart from the challenges and opportunities presented by creating a more inclusive student body, the new headmaster and his colleagues found themselves facing an unexpected concern. The annual budget for the new campus and its operations presumed an annual enrollment of 400 students or more, but by the early seventies enrollment had dipped below 370 with no immediate sign of a resurgence. Moreover it became increasingly clear in the aftermath of the divisive Vietnam War that the military dimension of the school's program was a problematic factor in attracting new applicants. Reducing or eliminating a program that had for more than a century been the defining feature of the school seemed at that time unthinkable to Chorpenning and Linsly's trustees. They were hopeful when the only other military school in West Virginia, the Greenbriar Military Academy in Lewisburg, closed its doors in 1972 that Linsly might absorb some of those families. Greenbriar had also offered Junior ROTC to its students, an Army-affiliated program in which high school boys received instruction in military science from regular Army instructors. Junior ROTC courses also conferred advanced standing to boys who went onto college officer training programs.

34 Linsly's Rifle Team and Drum and Bugle Corps Marching for President Carter's Inauguration, circa 1977

The incorporation of Junior ROTC would prove to be a mixed blessing for the Institute. The program required that the Army would provide three instructors, a colonel and two sergeants, whose pay would be supplemented by the school. The perceived difference in tone and substance between the Army instructors' classes and those taught by Linsly staff created an uneasy working relationship. Moreover, enrollment continued to decline through the mid-seventies to the extent that the school's operating expenses exceeded annual income. Concerned that the school right itself financially, Linsly trustees began casting about for a new headmaster with a proven financial and administrative acumen. Harry Chorpenning, admired and well-liked by his faculty colleagues, was encouraged to resume his post on the faculty but departed to teach at the junior college level.

As it happened, the search for an effective school leader proved to be protracted, casting the Institute's future course into considerable doubt. In consequence both faculty and boys were inclined to feel their school was adrift, its traditional standards not uniformly enforced. An editorialist in the November 5, 1974, issue of *The Cadet* posed the question to his fellow students: "What Are We—Barbarians?"

> Have you ever compared walking down a Linsly Hall to walking elsewhere? If you have, you would probably have to admit that nothing so aptly completes the comparison as does a zoo. With all the bumping and shoving and cursing going on, it is certainly hard to imagine that one is treading among humans.

The trustees appointed Ron Salvador (1950), to serve as Interim Headmaster for the 1976–77 school year. Salvador, a West Point graduate and retired Lieutenant Colonel in the U.S. Army, had served the school as Commandant of Cadets. As Salvador worked to maintain order and continuity, the board conducted a search for what they hoped would be a visionary and capable headmaster. By the spring of 1977 two promising candidates were identified, Reno DiOrio, the Assistant Headmaster of the Kiski School in Saltsburg, Pennsylvania, and Kenneth O. Kiesler, head of the newly founded Heritage School outside of Atlanta. Board Chairman Don Hofreuter recalled later that DiOrio was the trustees' enthusiastic first choice, but when the offer of appointment was made, DiOrio declined on the grounds that his current commitments to Kiski precluded leaving the school at that time. The positive impression DiOrio had made on Hofreuter and his trustee colleagues was such, however, that they would not soon forget him—a fact that would have profound consequences on the future of the school.

By the time Headmaster Kiesler assumed his duties in the fall of 1977, both the board and the faculty were aware that, despite its long tradition, the Linsly's military program had ceased to be an attractive factor for families considering the school. Kiesler himself had declined to assume a military rank or wear a uniform, thus breaking a century-long tradition. Required daily drills were reduced to twice a week, but admissions continued to decline. Even more ominous, there were mounting indications that Headmaster Kiesler and the Linsly community were not a satisfactory match. In the spring of 1978, with enrollments now dipping below 325 and considerable uncertainty about the direction of the school's leadership, a number of promising younger faculty members decided not to renew their contracts. Calls for structural changes in the school were countered by appeals to restore tradition and continuity. At decade's end it was clear that The Linsly Military Institute stood at a crossroads.

9 | A New Direction: The Arrival of Headmaster DiOrio

On a brisk Saturday morning in the autumn of 1978, the Kiski School football team bus pulled up the drive onto the Linsly campus in advance of that afternoon's scheduled game. Trustee Chairman Don Hofreuter had been waiting for that bus. When Kiski's football coach Reno DiOrio stepped out, Hofreuter greeted him and asked if they might take a walk while the team changed into their uniforms. As they strolled the campus, Hofreuter explained that the school was in serious need of new leadership and asked if DiOrio would be willing to talk further about the prospect of coming to Linsly. Before parting to ready his team for the game, DiOrio agreed to consider it.

Reflecting later, DiOrio recalled that back in 1977, when he was first approached by Linsly trustees about his possible candidacy as headmaster, he had not thought seriously about moving. In fact, he would have been unaware of the opening at Linsly had not Jack Pidgeon, Kiski's iconic headmaster, told him about it and urged him at least to meet with the Linsly people on the grounds that it would be a good experience for him to see what headmaster searches were like. Pidgeon felt reasonably certain that Linsly would not turn his young colleague's head. At age thirty-five, DiOrio had been a fast-rising star on the Kiski faculty, first as a heavily committed dormitory master, history teacher, and varsity coach. He and Karen and their three boys were happy in the close community of the boarding school.

Pidgeon's early hunch about his young protégé's promise proved correct. Both boys and colleagues quickly warmed to DiOrio as he progressed up through the school's administrative ranks, including the management of Kiski's extensive summer programs. He was elevated while still in his thirties to the assistant headmastership. Moreover, he seemed fully in the mold of a venerable cadre of Kiski staff members who had devoted lifelong careers to the school. Like many of them, DiOrio was a Kiski graduate (1959). And like many of them he had as a schoolboy been taken under Headmaster Pidgeon's wing and warmly supported as he made his way, first tentatively then impressively, as a scholar and an athlete.

Reno DiOrio grew up in semi-rural Burgettstown, Pennsylvania, twenty-five miles outside of Pittsburgh. Burgettstown was a working-class enclave where nearly everyone was employed in a steel mill or a related industrial factory. The DiOrios were a family of modest means, a condition strained when, at age twelve, Reno lost his father to a sudden illness. As he proceeded through the Burgettstown public schools, Reno's athletic promise began to attract local attention—but an attentive aunt who taught at the high school alerted the family that Reno lacked academic focus. Aware that her son's prospects for attending college were unlikely given his experience to date in Burgettstown, his mother drew on what savings she had to send Reno for a college preparatory senior year as a boarder at Kiski. DiOrio cannot recall another person in Burgettstown moving on to a college preparatory school.

Jack Pidgeon, then newly arrived from Deerfield Academy and just beginning his prodigious forty-six-year tenure as headmaster, took a liking to the hard-working and athletically talented new boy. After just six weeks of what DiOrio believed would be his senior year, Pidgeon summoned him to his office and told him that he wasn't really ready for a first-rate college yet—but could be if he stayed on at Kiski for another year. Aware that there were no family funds to pay for such a year, Pidgeon assured Reno's mother that her son could attend if she would agree to contribute "whatever she could"—a hundred dollars a month, twenty, nothing—toward his tuition. As Pidgeon predicted, the additional year enabled DiOrio to deepen himself scholastically, assume a leadership position among his fellow seniors, and lead strong football and baseball teams, achievements which won him admission to Dickinson College where he majored in psychology. A standout shortstop on Dickinson's baseball team and quarterback of its football team, he was inducted in 1978 into the college's Sports Hall of Fame. The tenacity, reliability, and affability that had marked his success at Kiski came into full bloom at Dickinson. By his senior year he had, in addition to his scholastic and athletic achievements, been named president of both the college's athletic council and of his fraternity, Phi Kappa Sigma, as well as to Dickinson's oldest and most exclusive honor society, Raven's Claw. The DiOrio legacy at Dickinson would be extended when Reno and Karen's oldest son David (Linsly, 1986), followed by their twins Matthew and Christopher (Linsly, 1988), entered the college. All three boys majored in English.

Throughout the summers of his high school and college years, DiOrio held a succession of jobs in Kiski's summer programs, jobs which helped put him through both institutions and which strengthened his ties to Headmaster Pidgeon, whose formative influence on DiOrio cannot be exaggerated. As DiOrio's graduation from Kiski approached in the spring of 1959, his headmaster once again summoned him to his study. This time the message was that when Reno completed his college education, he would be welcome back at Kiski as a teacher. DiOrio, who now regarded Kiski as no less than a second home, took the offer to heart. A graduate of Dickinson's Army ROTC program, he was committed to two years of military service following his graduation. As the Vietnam War loomed ominously, he was posted to a quiet station in Miami where his duties as a military psychologist were to administer mental tests to draftees. This was for DiOrio a remarkably painless assignment, enlivened briefly by an opportunity to test perhaps the most vocal antiwar draftee of the Vietnam era—Cassius Clay, soon to become Mohammad Ali.

Even more diverting than contending with Cassius Clay,[1] DiOrio met a hometown girl, Karen McCarrick, who had recently returned from a year in New York City to begin her undergraduate studies at Miami Dade Junior College. Reno and Karen were married in 1965, and when DiOrio's tour of duty was concluded in 1966, the newlyweds moved north to begin their new life together at the Kiski School in Saltsburg.

Not surprisingly, DiOrio acknowledges Pidgeon as the single-most influential person—after his mother—in his life, an influence that would shape DiOrio's approach to school mastering first at Kiski and then at Linsly. This approach—by no means typical and far from standard practice—has venerable origins in the history of independent schools in the United States. The great American independent schools—the Phillips Academies at Exeter and Andover, Lawrenceville, Groton, Hotchkiss, Deerfield—came to prominence due either to inspired founders or headmasters of long tenure who articulated and carried out a clear and distinctive vision of how they believed school should be kept. These visionaries were not notably collaborative, nor did they require colleagues' or parents' or anybody else's consensus in order to proceed. School leaders like Endicott Peabody of Groton, Father Sill of Kent, Roger Drury of St. Paul's, and Frank Boyden of Deerfield articulated the missions of their schools and personally saw to it that those missions were realized.[2] They directed daily school business personally and intimately.

Hofreuter's appeal to reconsider the Linsly headmastership this time intrigued DiOrio and his wife Karen. That fall and winter he did his best to learn the practical circumstances bearing on the Institute's present situation. He was aware that the admissions picture was at best cloudy and that the school's financial position had weakened over the 1970s. His greatest misgiving, however, was about the school's military program. It was not simply that the martial ethos did not appeal to him; he could not see a way for the school as constituted to rebound in the post-Vietnam era. When he made these observations known, Hofreuter proposed that DiOrio accept the post and then conduct a two- or three-year review of whether the military program should be retained. DiOrio suggested an alternative course: that the trustees and current staff of the Institute, those with the deepest knowledge and commitment to the school, determine whether to retain

A New Direction: The Arrival of Headmaster DiOrio

or dissolve the military program—and when that decision was made, *then* search for the headmaster best suited to the type of school that remained.

So advised, Hofreuter and his fellow trustees deliberated about the future of the military program. A special session of the full board was convened in which all views, pro and con, were aired. At that session the board also solicited the opinions of retired Col. Lockhart, Captain Douglas Haigwood, and Captain James Hawkins who was director of admissions, all three of whom recommended dropping the military program and establishing Linsly as a conventional college preparatory school. After due deliberation the board formally adopted this position, the change to commence with the 1979–80 school year. The issue now settled, DiOrio was offered the headmastership of the new Linsly. On Christmas Eve, 1978, in the course of exchanging holiday good wishes over the telephone, DiOrio told Hofreuter he would be pleased to accept the position.

When Hofreuter addressed the assembled school to announce the decision to terminate the military program, the cadets, while surprised, were cautiously favorable to the change. Linsly's last Cadet Major and *The Cadet* editor-in-chief Scott Bond wrote in a March 1979 editorial that "the termination of the military tradition at Linsly ends a once rewarding 100 year era. No longer will students don the gray and black, worry about a lost name plate, or hurry to morning inspection." Bond went on to say that in recent years the military program had been "tolerated" as a required dimension of an otherwise strong academic experience. About the prospects for the school's future, Bond expressed optimism. "Linsly will remain the finest institution for secondary schooling in the three-state area, and perhaps under the skillful leadership of Mr. DiOrio be unequalled anywhere. Forward Linsly and no re. . . I mean onward, onward." Today Bond continues to serve the school as a trustee.

35 Scott S. Bond, the Last Cadet Major Class of 1979

The editorial staff of the 1979 yearbook, *At Ease*, largely concurred with Bond, cautioning the rising underclassmen "to remember that the philosophy of this educational institution . . . will continue to stress self-discipline, leadership, and academic excellence. Uniform dress, gentlemanly conduct and real effort will be expected of every Linsly student."

Later that spring, on the morning of May 24, under lowering skies and a forecast of rain, the Linsly Battalion impressively carried out its last Final Drills in full dress before a stadium of parents, friends, and other supporters of the school. The boys were not unmoved by the finality of the ceremony. "By 8:30, it was all over," an *At Ease* editorialist wrote, "and in our hearts we were quite proud and self-satisfied that, despite adversity, we had done our best in our final show of true character and student body esprit. A job well done, and our *final* Final Drills, *en fin,* was a tribute to us all."

Throughout that winter and spring the headmaster-elect worked hard to acquaint himself with his new colleagues and to establish a set of priorities that would bring the school back into equilibrium after nearly a decade of changing leadership. As expected, a contingent of loyal alumni was disheartened by the termination of the military program, in effect drawing a close to what had been "their" Linsly. DiOrio was relieved, however, that the remaining faculty did not seem resistant to the change and in fact many of them were, like him, hopeful that this new iteration of the school would restore its sagging fortunes.

The mid-century had not been a prosperous period for Wheeling and surrounding towns. As steel and coal production declined in the region, supporting businesses and services failed to prosper. From a peak of nearly 62,000 in 1930, Wheeling's population had declined by 1980 to 43,000, a trend that has continued precipitously; the 2010 census listed the city's population at 28,486. At the millennium, median family income had dropped to $27,388, with 18 percent of the population living below the federally established poverty line. Reinvigorating a fee-charging, independent school in this economic climate was clearly going to be a challenge.

Despite the attrition of discouraged younger faculty that preceded DiOrio's arrival, the school could still demonstrate a number of critical strengths. Primary among them was that the Linsly student body was scholastically able, their measured performance and college placement record unrivalled in the Ohio Valley. The school's academic program was well-considered and rigorous, and the athletic program was solid. DiOrio's personal challenge, as he reflected later, was to convince an understandably skeptical faculty that *this* new headmaster—a thirty-seven-year-old headmaster at that—meant to immerse himself fully in the life of the school, to follow through on his stated intentions, and to *stay*.

On the eve of the first day of school in the late summer of 1979, Headmaster DiOrio invited the faculty and their spouses to his campus home for a dinner reception, to be followed by a brief faculty meeting. DiOrio remembers wanting to accomplish two things: to convey a clear sense of what he believed an independent school could be at its best and to allay any fears that the post-military Linsly would lack discipline. For in fact DiOrio had learned a thing or two about student accountability at Kiski, where boys were required to be well groomed, clean shaven, and wear coats and ties throughout the academic day. Kiski boys were in addition expected to address their teachers and one another respectfully, to respect one another's possessions, and generally to deport themselves as gentlemen. DiOrio's personal inclination as he assumed his new duties was to *raise* expectations for discipline and decorum at Linsly. But whatever his intentions as he stood to address his colleagues at the outset of his first year as headmaster, he was not at all certain he would be taken seriously. He remembers scanning the faces of the faculty as he spoke and feeling that they looked "puzzled," which did little to boost his confidence. As he concluded his inaugural remarks he did not know what to think. At which point Don Clutter, a veteran of the English faculty and a highly respected teacher, rose to his feet and began to applaud. Clutter was immediately joined by the rest of the faculty, a show of support and goodwill DiOrio remembers with special gratitude to this day.

The close attention of trustees Ogden Nutting, Fred Stamp, and Don Hofreuter proved to be essential in the successful transition of leadership. Even before the DiOrios arrived in Wheeling, Hofreuter hosted a series of dinners that enabled the new headmaster to meet board members and faculty. With continued support from Clutter, Athletic Director Eugene "Eudie" Joseph, and other seasoned Linsly staff, DiOrio began to chart the school's course for the new decade.

36 Dr. Don Hofreuter, Trustee Chairman from 1975 to 2010

37 Ogden Nutting, currently an emeritus trustee, has served on the Linsly board since 1975.

38 The Honorable Frederick P. Stamp, currently an emeritus trustee, has served on the Linsly board since 1975.

NOTES

1. By 1965 Cassius Clay was already a national celebrity due to his triumphs as an Olympic boxer. The reason he was assigned to Miami for testing is that he was already in training there for his historic first match with heavyweight champion Sonny Liston, a bout he would go on to win. As might be expected, Clay passed his Army physical with ease, but the mental ability tests DiOrio administered proved to be a problem, as Clay's scores were below the accepted level for service. Whether due to poor instruction and little scholastic motivation when he was a schoolboy

in Louisville, Kentucky, or to his resistance to serving the Vietnam War effort—he would later tell the press, "I ain't got nothin' against those Viet Cong." Clay's failure to pass the Army's test of mental competence caused something of a national stir. Urged by Congress, the Department of the Army conducted an investigation of how someone as physically vigorous and occasionally eloquent as Clay could not be found fit to serve. At length Clay was retested in Louisville, with similar results, and was relegated to "trainability limited" status, which made it highly unlikely that he would be called to duty. For his part, Lieutenant DiOrio felt vindicated that his test assessments were confirmed and supported by his superiors—and rather dazzled to have made the acquaintance of one of the premier athletes in boxing history.

2 Deerfield's Boyden was the exemplar of the type. The virtual founder of Deerfield Academy, he transformed a failing village school in western Massachusetts into perhaps the premier American boarding school, its practices admired and imitated across the country. Boyden was headmaster of Deerfield for sixty-six years, a length of tenure not only unrivaled but barely approached. Boyden placed his working desk, unenclosed by walls, in the busy center of the main school building. He saw every boy in the school every day. He looked after every school detail from the design of school sports uniforms to dining hall menus. Without aid of handbook or any other formal protocols he conducted all faculty and student business personally. There was no written conduct code. There was admirable discipline, but it was administered personally and fluidly, as he felt circumstances warranted. In sixty-six years, Boyden expelled almost nobody. Eccentric, phenomenally determined, and unimposing in his outward manner, he was the length and shadow of his school. In 1966 Deerfield alumnus and Pulitzer Prize–winning author John McPhee wrote a short and highly regarded biography of Boyden, *The Headmaster*, in which he concluded that in his tenacity and in the depth of his personal commitment to his school, he was nothing short of a great man.

10 | The Road to Coeducation

As the school proceeded into the 1979–80 school year, Headmaster DiOrio and the board were reassured that while applications for admission did not immediately increase in consequence of dropping the military program, there was no exodus of families disappointed by the change. Gradually, however, beginning the following year, new interest was kindled in what was still the region's leading college preparatory school, thanks in good measure to the energetic outreach into the community by Admissions Director Jim Hawkins. In the uncertain years prior to the appointment of the new headmaster, enrollment had dipped to as low as 280 boys, worryingly below the 400 figure upon which the school calculated its annual operating budget when the new campus was completed.

From the boys' standpoint, the post-military prospects were bright. The consensus among the students was that the new headmaster and his staff were creating a forward-looking,

39 Jim Hawkins, Admissions Director, circa 1982

positive momentum. At the conclusion of DiOrio's inaugural year, the staff of the 1980 yearbook, renamed *Linsly Log*, opined that "under a new administration the school looks up with a new kind of hope... Linsly's future is brighter than ever with the "look" [the students' term for the new, post-military dress code], the Prefect system, and the administration all working for the good of the school... We certainly are turning over a New Leaf!"

Kevin Stevick (1980), who had entered Linsly as a tenth grade cadet in 1977, recalls the experience of studying under three successive headmasters—Salvador, Kiesler, and DiOrio—in as many years. Students were aware, he felt, of the uncertainty accompanying both the termination of the military program and the arrival of a new administration. The transition was eased, he believes, by the melding of the former system of military-based student leadership to the prefectorial system installed to replace it. Like the military hierarchy of student command, the prefect system advanced upperclassmen to leadership positions based on a system of points earned for academic performance, extracurricular performance, and good conduct. Under the military system, Stevick stood to assume the position of Cadet Major, qualifications for which made him Head Prefect the first year of the new system. Stevick would go on from Linsly to study at Annapolis, returning to the school's service in 2007 as a trustee. In May 2014 he was named chairman of the board.

40 Kevin Stevick, circa 1980, Linsly's First Head Prefect and Chairman of the Linsly Board of Trustees, May 2014

Sensitive to the fact that very few African American boys were enrolled, mostly boarders from Steubenville and Columbus, DiOrio wasted no time building connections to old Pittsburgh-area friends who ran summer camps and recreational programs for minority children. The subsequent stream of African American students entering the school from Pittsburgh included an athletically talented young man named Willie Clay (1988). An excellent basketball and baseball player, Clay had little football experience prior to entering Linsly, but he would soon become a standout on Linsly teams as well as an overall solid student. In all, Clay earned twelve varsity letters over the course of his high school years before going on to Georgia Tech where, among many other accomplishments, he intercepted sixteen passes in a single season, breaking the school record of fourteen. Although standing only five foot nine and weighing 180 pounds, Clay was drafted by the Detroit Lions as a cornerback where he enjoyed three successful seasons in the defensive secondary and was subsequently traded to the New England Patriots, closing his career with the New Orleans Saints.

Willie Clay, like many of the boys personally recruited to the school by DiOrio, has continued to hold his Linsly years in affectionate regard. Clay has established a permanent scholarship in his name and continues to correspond with his old headmaster, who attended his wedding and business grand opening in Atlanta. Another early African American standout at Linsly was David Rose (1984). A Brooklyn native, Rose compiled an impressive scholastic record at Linsly and went on to Princeton. A fervent and knowledgeable sports maven while he was at Linsly, he was urged by Headmaster DiOrio to make the acquaintance of Bill Grimes (1959), then president of ESPN, whom DiOrio had invited to address the student body. Rose enthusiastically complied, and as a result of their continuing acquaintance Rose was hired by the network. Grimes too has been a loyal friend to the school. In 2011 he endowed a student scholarship in Karen and Reno DiOrio's honor.

Sobered by demographic projections that both population and family income in the region were likely to decline, DiOrio, like his predecessor Guy Holden in the thirties, energetically established his presence—and with it Linsly's presence—in the community, with modest but encouraging results. In each successive year enrollment increased, to 320, 325, then 350. Many of the newly recruited students were boarders. When DiOrio arrived on campus, the number of boarding students had declined to 40; with renewed recruiting efforts, the number climbed steadily back up to 100, enough to warrant a new dormitory and needed renovations of the older facilities. Nonetheless, by mid-decade it was clear that dramatic further increases in enrollment were unlikely to occur in the absence of some unforeseen development or a structural change.

One such change, a profound and potentially divisive one, would be to open admission to girls—in Linsly's case, a reversion to the school's practice prior to the Civil War. To do so would hardly be a novelty in the

41 Reno DiOrio with Students, circa 1989

current educational climate. Over the course of the previous two decades many single-sex independent schools, including practically all the nation's leading boarding schools, had gone coed: Exeter (1970), St. Paul's and Hotchkiss (1971), Andover (1973), Choate (1974), and the trend finally capped by Lawrenceville (1985) and Deerfield (1989). Closer to home, Cleveland's Western Reserve Academy had begun admitting girls in 1972, followed the next year by Pittsburgh's Shady Side Academy. The all-boys composition of Linsly was clearly close to the hearts of its graduates—and to many of the faculty. But the fact remained that to be an all-boys school in the closing years of the millennium was to risk appearing anachronistic.

It was apparent by the mid-1980s that Mount de Chantal, once a distinctive and highly regarded Catholic girls' school, was failing to thrive. Both boarding and day student enrollment had fallen precipitously. As trustees and faculty began an open consideration of admitting girls, the abiding questions were whether the likely increase in enrollment would justify the related capital improvements necessary to accommodate a coed student body—and more fundamentally, would a coed Linsly be a better school? DiOrio was determined to answer both questions. Like many of his faculty and like Admissions Director Hawkins, DiOrio had worked only in boys' schools—and was a strong advocate of the form. Even if persuaded that a coed Linsly would prove to be a better school, DiOrio wanted to make sure he knew how to negotiate what was for him unexplored scholastic territory before a decisive and irreversible commitment was made.

In the course of the 1986–87 school year DiOrio and a team of his administrative colleagues visited a series of schools that had made the conversion from all-boys to coeducation. These visitations included Western Reserve Academy, Shady Side Academy, Mercersburg Academy, the Lawrenceville School, and the Baylor School. DiOrio also arranged visits and consultations with his alma mater, Kiski, and with other schools that had considered coeducation but decided to remain single-sex. Of the schools visited, the Baylor School in Chattanooga, Tennessee, represented the closest model to Linsly. Formerly an all-boys military academy, Baylor had first abandoned its military program (1971) and then converted to coeducation (1985). In the course of a three-day immersion in the Baylor School's culture, DiOrio was able to talk freely to Dr. Herbert Barks, the headmaster, as well as to faculty, staff, boys, and parents. DiOrio recalls an especially telling incident Dr. Barks shared with him about persuading resistant alums of the practical necessity of coeducation. Barks apparently minced no words with Baylor graduates, telling them that they could either have fond memories of the school of their boyhood or they could have a school that continued to exist—but they could not have both. Today Baylor enrolls over a thousand boys and girls in grades six through twelve. Its students annually lead the South in Advanced Placement test performance, and its athletic program, for both boys and girls, continues to dominate state competition in Tennessee.

Heartened by what he learned at Baylor, DiOrio also received what he realized later was an invaluable tip from Shady Side Headmaster Emerson Johnson. Whereas most schools and colleges converted to coeducation by yearly admitting girls to one class at a time until all classes were composed of boys and girls, Johnson strongly advised admitting girls to all classes simultaneously—and as many as possible. Doing so would help the pioneering first female attendees to not feel like a hothouse novelty in a predominantly male institution. DiOrio was determined not to create an outwardly coeducational school that felt to its students "like a boys' school with girls in it."

The looming prospect of a coeducational Linsly raised a number of concerns on the part of the school's constituents. From the outset of the 1987–88 school year, administrators and faculty met continuously with current parents, prospective parents, alumni, and faculty, not so much to persuade them of the value of admitting girls as to learn what they thought and felt about it. Prominent among the concerns expressed was the ability of the Linsly faculty to teach and otherwise provide appropriate nurture and guidance to girls. The costs of needed alterations to the plant and program were also a significant factor in deciding to move forward. A new girls' dormitory would have to be built. Locker rooms and adjustments

The Road to Coeducation

to the athletic facilities would have to be provided. Uncountable adjustments to the athletic and scholastic program would have to be made.

Recalling the unhelpfully protracted deliberations that preceded the Institute's decision to end the military program, Board Chairman Hofreuter and his fellow trustees were determined to take this next major step decisively. Late in the autumn of 1987, the board resolved not only to admit girls to the school, but also to offer them places in all but the junior and senior classes for the coming school year. This would leave a little more than six months to ready the school for coeducation—a process that typically busied schools for two or three years. What followed was something of a whirlwind of meetings and deliberations ranging from curriculum changes to streamlining the construction of a new dormitory and new physical education locker rooms in Banes Hall. Other, highly specific considerations had to be determined. What, for example, should be the required girls' school uniform? After considerable deliberation, the school's administrative team determined that the girls' dress code should mirror that of the boys' as closely as possible. With the termination of the military program and required military dress, it was made clear that Linsly boys would continue to wear a school uniform and that it would be suitably decorous: blazers and ties, slacks that were not blue jeans, and dress shoes. The dress code specified for the girls would be blazers and ties, plain blouses, a gray or plaid skirt, knee socks or tights, loafers or flats. For considerations of warmth and comfort, some faculty felt the girls might be allowed to wear suitable slacks, a variation that would not be adopted for another decade.

42 Cheryl Sprague and Jim Hawkins with Linsly students who were the first female candidates for enrollment. From left to right are Samantha Perin, Jennifer Yoon, and Janice Shellhase.

In an effort to ease the faculty's concerns about pedagogy appropriate to girls, two professors from West Virginia University's education department were invited to conduct a daylong workshop with Linsly's staff. Well-received by the faculty overall, the professors' discussion of gender-based differences in the way boys and girls respond in mixed classes included the observation that boys tended to be more impulsive in offering opinions or answering questions, girls more deliberate, taking time to consider if what they had to say merited saying. This finding, strongly supported by subsequent studies over the course of the following decade, invited teachers to resist acknowledging the first person to speak up or raise a hand and instead to pause for a suitable period of reflection before entertaining responses to a question. If not, the faculty was cautioned, boys would end up doing 90 percent of the talking in a typical class. Other pedagogical adjustments would have to be improvised as the girls arrived.

43 Linsly's First Girls Varsity Soccer Team, circa 1996

The move to coeducation necessitated the creation of a girls' athletic program, one that would soon take its place alongside the traditionally strong boys' program. The limited availability of female coaches cast men as coaches of most of the girls' teams, a role most assumed in a spirit of discovery and goodwill. Reflecting back, DiOrio recalls that most of the male coaches of female teams established positive relations with their players, although he remembers one father who was more than a little upset when his daughter was advised by her male coach that the necessary quickness required of her on the basketball team would involve losing weight.

Perhaps the busiest office in the school during the half-year scramble to ready Linsly for the arrival of girls was the admissions office. Jim Hawkins and his staff presided over extensive new admissions testing dates, orientation sessions for families of girls considering Linsly, and new student interviews. Mindful of Emerson Johnson's caveat to admit a sizable enough cohort of girls to create an all-school climate in which they felt substantial and secure, DiOrio and Hawkins were pleased to be able to grant admission to 65 girls for the fall of the 1988–89 school year, boosting overall enrollment to nearly 400, an encouraging indication of capacity-straining enrollments of 450, which followed in the 1990s.

As the conversion to coeducation approached, fears and concerns—that girls would somehow diminish academic expectations, that girls' leadership opportunities would be overshadowed by more aggressive boys, that boys' and girls' interests in one another would weaken academic focus and rigor—were decisively allayed almost from the outset. Girls' scholastic averages have typically exceeded that of the boys. Standards and expectations for both boys and girls have remained high, and, far from being relegated to lesser roles in the school, since

The Road to Coeducation

the onset of coeducation in 1988 girls have earned the top student leadership position, Head Prefect, more often than boys.

As the school readied itself for the arrival of its first female students in over a century, the boys were generally positive about the change, though aware that their school would be fundamentally transformed. In a thoughtful editorial statement published in the 1988 yearbook, now titled simply *Linsly*, a graduating editor mused that "the attitude of the student body will also have to change. Many believe that an environment that contains both boys and girls can only be for the better, not only because it will broaden the student body's outlook, but also because it will create a more realistic atmosphere, one in which Linsly students will live in the future."

The banging and hammering of carpenters, the roaring and sputtering of construction vehicles readying the campus for the coming girls—a new dormitory, an expanded gymnasium, the addition of new locker facilities—punctuated school life through the spring of 1988. Even before the girls arrived, students were oriented to a new dress code, a new administrative structure, including the central role of Cheryl Sprague as Upper School academic dean and designated guardian angel of the entering girls.

And then they arrived. Wendy McAtee, a new boarder from Western Pennsylvania, wrote "Linsly co-ed at last!" in a lead article in the newly formatted school newspaper, *The Linsly Line*. "I looked forward to school all summer, and now I am delighted to be here. Being one of the first girl graduates in over one hundred and forty years will definitely be an honor." (Two years later she would indeed graduate, with highest honors.) The initial hesitance she experienced on the part of both boys and girls in the initial days of the 1988–89 school year felt to her "like an elementary school dance where the girls stand by one wall and the boys stand by the other wall." But as she and her new schoolmates of both genders got to know each other, the hesitancy dissolved. "Well, I have to say that Linsly pulled it off," she concluded. "Everyone is doing his and her best to make things work smoothly."

The launch of the 1988–89 school year was also brightened by the addition of a new outdoor wilderness dimension to the standard school program. On Saturday, October 28, the Linsly Outdoor Center (LOC) was dedicated at Raccoon Creek State Park in Hookstown, Pennsylvania. The day of the dedication boys and girls demonstrated for invited guests how they could work together to meet various physical challenges while building teamwork, leadership, and trust. The new

44 Jeff Hasis with Students at the Linsly Outdoor Center

thirty-acre facility included two dormitories, a dining hall, an administration building, and a nature center, to which the school would add a twenty-element ropes course. Today Linsly students participate in LOC activities in the course of each successive school year. There are opportunities for leadership development and individual skill-building as students experience rock climbing, white water rafting, camping, backpacking, and ecological field work. After a quarter century the LOC has become a defining element in every Linsly graduate's experience.

Throughout the decade the school's daily program of scholastic and physical challenges was leavened by periodic special programs featuring guest artists, public servants, writers, and other notables. In February 1995 Linsly invited back one of its graduates, Jack Canfield (1962), coauthor with Mark Victor Hansen of the best-selling inspirational book, *Chicken Soup for the Soul* (1993). Today one of the nation's leading motivational speakers, Canfield proceeded from Linsly to Harvard for his undergraduate studies and then to the University of Massachusetts for a master's degree in education. His subsequent work as a teacher and therapist evolved into a program of highly successful seminars on self-esteem. The initial *Chicken Soup* book was followed by a string of successful sequels and related consumer products still marketed worldwide today. In what the 1995 yearbook editors considered the year's most inspiring guest presentation, Canfield shared stories of ordinary Americans who achieved extraordinary things through persistence and determination—and urged Linsly students to do likewise.

45 Jack Canfield with Linsly Prefects, circa 1995

From the standpoint of all of its constituents, coeducational Linsly was experiencing a new vibrancy. In a November 1989 editorial in *The Linsly Line* Brad Naranch marveled at what, in just a year, seemed to him a much *bigger* school. Now enrolling 391 students, including 99 boarders, the Linsly student body had grown 13 percent larger than the previous year's bumper crop. The editorial attributed the admissions boom to two clear factors: the school's distinctive scholastic profile and that so many parents in the region were eager for their daughters to have an opportunity to attend. Naranch's article concludes with an observation also made at year's end by the yearbook staff: that attendance at games and dances and other school outings had increased dramatically with the arrival of girls.

Given the realities of declining population and income in the region, Linsly's emergence as a viable, vibrant, and *growing* school is a testament both to the vision of DiOrio, now in full command after nearly a decade at his post, and to Board Chairman Hofreuter and his fellow trustees.

11 | A New Coherence: Linsly Through the Nineties

Despite the hurried arrangements to ready the school for its newly enrolled girls, Linsly managed what for many schools proved to be a problematic transition with considerable grace. This was due in good part to DiOrio and his administrative team's thoughtful research into how coeducation was successfully introduced elsewhere. The adjusted administrative structure for the coeducational school would consist of Headmaster DiOrio, Assistant Headmaster Terry Depew, Upper School Dean John Whitehead, Lower School Dean Gary Sprague, and Academic Dean of the Upper School Cheryl Sprague.

The school's positive momentum from the outset of coeducation can be attributed to the shared commitment of a faculty and staff energized by

46 Cheryl Sprague, Academic Dean of the Upper School, circa 1997

what they perceived as a reassuring stability and sense of purpose on the part of the school's leadership. This heartening momentum owed a great deal to veteran Linsly faculty who stood fast and supported the new headmaster when the school's fortunes were at best cloudy. Prominent among the veteran staff who saw the school through its two definitive structural changes—the termination of the military program and the admission of girls—were Gary and Cheryl Sprague, Don Clutter, Eudie Joseph, Jim Hawkins, and Denny Hon.

Gary Sprague has been Linsly's longest serving faculty member. Upon completion of his BA in English and history at West Virginia Wesleyan College and his MA in education at West Virginia University, he was appointed to Linsly's Middle School faculty to teach English and classics courses in the fall of 1968. He ascended to the Middle School deanship in 1973 and has presided over Linsly's younger learners for forty-one years. His many coaching responsibilities have included a remarkable thirty-four-year stint as head varsity baseball coach, a span which included a 488–253 win-loss record, thirteen Ohio Valley Athletic Conference championships and, in 2012, induction into the OVAC Hall of Fame. Cheryl Sprague also matriculated through West Virginia Wesleyan (BA in Education) and West Virginia University (MA in Curriculum and Structure). She directed the education program of Wheeling's Florence Crittenton House, a state-supported shelter for pregnant and troubled girls before joining Linsly's Upper School English department in 1984. As the prospect of coeducation became a reality, she was named to the newly appointed post of Upper School academic dean with the understanding that she would preside over the integration of girls into the school's program, an assignment that, by all accounts, she has carried out masterfully. The Sprague's three children, Don, Doug, and Jaclyn, graduated from Linsly in 1989, 1992, and 1995, respectively. A number of teachers who served over the course of the DiOrio years have commented that the most satisfying dimension of their work was the feeling that the combined faculty felt more like an extended *family* than it did a cluster

47 Gary Sprague, Dean of the Lower School, circa 1980

48 Don Clutter, English Department, circa 1980

of working colleagues. For nearly a half century the Spragues were a central fixture in that family constellation.

Don Clutter, who had led the standing ovation for his new headmaster on the occasion of DiOrio's inaugural talk to the faculty, was a masterful teacher of English throughout the 1960s, 1970s, and 1980s. He was a central figure in the lives of his students, remembered both for his command of great literature and his emphasis on a strong grounding in the fundamentals of correct usage. Eudie Joseph began his Linsly career in the autumn of 1952. A career-long history teacher and coach, he represented the athletic heart of the school. A star basketball player on the University of Dayton's perennially strong Flyers, he would go on to coach highly successful basketball teams at Linsly, also serving as head track coach and assisting with the football program. Later in his career he served the school as athletic director, revered by his students and players for his depth of commitment to the school and to them personally. When he retired in 1987, he had been a central element in Linsly life for thirty-five years.

Among a staunch cohort of long-serving teachers, none could boast a deeper connection to Linsly than Jim Hawkins. Hawkins was reared in Pittsburgh. His father

49 Eudie Joseph, Athletic Director, circa 1991

passed away when Jim was twelve, and in the aftermath his mother enrolled him as a boarder in Linsly's eighth grade. Through his high school years he distinguished himself as a fine all-around athlete and a standout on perennially strong football teams. Following four years at West Virginia Wesleyan College where he once again distinguished himself as a scholar athlete, Hawkins returned to Linsly in 1962 where he taught physical education, instructed marksmen on the rifle range, and helped coach football, basketball, and track teams, eventually emerging as the Orange and Black's head football coach. In the troubled period in the mid-1970s, Hawkins was asked to step in to fill a critical vacancy in the admissions office. In that post he became a crucial factor in the school's resurgence, not merely finding and admitting students, but maintaining an interest in each of them as they progressed through the school. Hawkins would serve the school as admissions director until the brink of his retirement when he oriented his younger colleague, Chad Barnett, to take over the admissions operation. Except for his four years as an undergraduate, Hawkins studied and then served at Linsly for a remarkable forty-nine years.

Bob Reeves began his Linsly teaching career under Lockhart in 1962 and rose to become the chairman of the social studies department, a post he held for more than twenty years. He was the guiding light of the school's forensics program, coaching speech and debate and organizing the Junior Town Meeting, a debate competition among selected regional schools. He served also as Linsly's tennis coach for most of his career. He retired in 2001 after nearly four decades of service.

In 1977, Denny Hon, a gifted young teacher of mathematics, left the Linsly faculty in frustration at what he felt was a lack of direction in the school's operation. He was teaching in the math department

50 Bob Reeves, Head of the History Department, circa 1987

51 Denny Hon, Head of the Math Department, circa 1998

at Wheeling Park High School when his former colleagues apprised new Headmaster DiOrio that the school had lost a gem and that it would be a wonderful thing to have him back. DiOrio duly sought out Hon and negotiated his return—to the enduring satisfaction of more than three decades of Linsly scholars. Chairman of the school's math department and for years a reader and grader of the nationally administered Advanced Placement examinations, Hon has guided Linsly math students to consistent success on their AP tests. A notebook he composed for his advanced calculus students is now formally printed by the school. It is a document Linsly graduates treasure for easing their passage through demanding college-level mathematics courses. Hon announced his retirement at the conclusion of the 2012–13 school year, a milestone very close to the heart of Linsly's bicentennial celebration.

Appointed to the Linsly faculty by Basil Lockhart in 1967, Margaret Ragni—affectionately known as "Frau" Ragni by her students over the course of four decades—was until her retirement in 1994 one of the school's most respected teachers. A long-time chair of the Foreign Languages Department, she was the principal teacher of German while occasionally teaching courses in Latin and English. Her German scholars were consistent winners in German language competitions statewide and nationally. Celebrated roundly on the occasion of her retirement, she would continue to offer part-time help in the Banes Hall library.

To the faculty and staff he inherited DiOrio added a succession of men and women who would themselves become central fixtures in the school. In 1974 while he was still at Kiski, DiOrio was on the lookout for a new math teacher who could also coach football.

When Terry Depew, a young scholar athlete freshly out of Bucknell University (BS, MS), showed up to interview, he was hired on the spot. He quickly established himself as a fine mathematics teacher and coach at Kiski, and in 1978 when DiOrio was due to leave and assume leadership at Linsly, Depew and his wife, Cathy, decided to leave Kiski as well, as Terry had hopes of relocating closer to his native central Pennsylvania. Since Linsly was at the time looking for a new business manager, it occurred to DiOrio that the mathematically astute Depew might fill the bill—a staffing gamble that in the years ahead proved prescient, as Depew quickly acquired the financial and accounting acumen necessary to steer

52 Margaret "Frau" Ragni, Foreign Language Department, circa 1986

53 Terry C. Depew, Head Football Coach for Twenty-six Successful Seasons

the school through its annual operational cycle. Today Depew recalls that the school's financial records, including its billing and bill paying procedures, were in considerable disarray. With patient and much appreciated help from trustee treasurer Robert Hazlett, the Linsly books were systematically put right. In addition to his duties in the business office, Depew would continue to teach mathematics, succeeding Jim Hawkins in 1980 as the head varsity football coach, a position he held with distinction for twenty-seven years. Later, as DiOrio's Assistant Headmaster, Depew would emerge as a masterful listener and mediator of faculty concerns. Like her husband, Cathy Depew had also made a bright start at Kiski, serving its development office, work she would continue at Linsly before becoming DiOrio's personal assistant, a position she continues to hold since DiOrio assumed the post of president upon his retirement as headmaster. The Depew's son, B.J., graduated from Linsly in 1995 and, after completing his BA at Ohio State in 1999, returned to his alma mater to teach mathematics. An apple fallen not far from the tree, B.J. is now head football coach of the Orange and Black. Reflecting back, DiOrio readily confesses that he could not imagine carrying out his duties at Linsly over the decades without the friendship and support of the Depews.

In addition to Terry Depew, DiOrio would bring with him from Kiski another masterful teacher. In 1979 when Karen DiOrio began to imagine her new life in Wheeling—a city that she recalls seemed "like Paris"

54 Karen and Reno DiOrio, circa 1982

compared to the tiny riverside hamlet of Saltsburg, Pennsylvania—the prospect of teaching had not entered her mind. When she and Reno were married in Miami in 1965, she had not yet completed her undergraduate studies. At Kiski the arrival of sons David (1967) and twins Matt and Chris (1969) commanded her attention as the DiOrios assumed the uncountable *in loco parentis* responsibilities of boarding school faculty couples. In Wheeling, as her sons entered their teenage years, Karen enrolled in a bachelors degree program at West Liberty

College (now West Liberty University), concentrating on elementary education and child development. Upon the completion of her BA in 1984, she was invited to fill a social studies opening in the Linsly middle school where she quickly became a valued and highly distinctive teacher of history and western hemisphere geography. Remembered fondly and much visited by Linsly boys and girls long after they ascended out of the middle school, Karen brought assigned lessons to life through a number of unforgettable gestures. She would appear in class from time to time dressed as the historical figure under study, and she would take pains that her students did not merely read about historical events but would also *experience* them. Thus, to help her classes understand the American colonists' mounting agitation as they paid taxes levied by a British parliament in which they were unrepresented, she would "tax" them—charge them pennies and nickels for the lead in their pencils and other school supplies—until the point was grasped. Even after her retirement from teaching in 2005, Karen DiOrio's former students greet her with the slogan, "No taxation without representation!"

Before he assumed his new duties at Linsly, DiOrio had been impressed by the school's scholastic rigor and its robust athletic program. But he was a seasoned enough school veteran to know that good schools are more dimensional than that. The Institute's long tradition of minstrels and then annual Extravaganzas had provided an enlivening creative outlet for the former cadets, but more would be needed for a different kind of student body in a different era. DiOrio, who had trusted his instincts before in hiring teachers fresh out of college, elected to do so again when he interviewed a fledgling Frank Wilson

55 Frank Wilson, Chairman of the Fine Arts Department, circa 2006

in 1980 for an opening in the music department. Utterly untried, the newly graduated young man from West Chester University in eastern Pennsylvania would, over the following four decades, come to define the musical and artistic life of the school. In DiOrio's estimation "the most creative person on our faculty," Wilson today serves as chairman of the Fine Arts Department, director of upper and lower school music programs, director of stage productions, including the Extravaganzas and—because he is technologically adept—the school's webmaster. His colleagues are quick to state they cannot imagine the school without him.

The Linsly Fine Arts Department was further graced by another 1980 college graduate, Dan Buchwach. Fresh out of Edinboro University, Buchwach represented an unusual combination of athleticism and aestheticism, and in the fall of 1980 began teaching studio art classes while helping to coach in both the football and track programs. When Eudie Joseph retired as athletic director in 1989, Buchwach was named athletic director. For years a central fixture in the school's residential life, Buchwach continues to teach studio art and art appreciation.

56 Mark Zavatsky and Dan Buchwach Honored at the 2014 Athletic Ceremony

An impressive West Virginia University swimmer, Bill Brubaker was hired by DiOrio in 1980 to teach social studies and to coach swimming. Flourishing in both roles, Brubaker went on to chair

57 Bill Brubaker, Social Studies Department, circa 1994

the Social Studies Department and to take over varsity swim coach responsibilities. The remarkable success of his swim teams was acknowledged by OVAC in 2012 when they named the annual swim championships the Bill Brubaker Meet. Like the other "rookies" who began their teaching careers in 1980, Brubaker has joined the ranks of career-long Linsly contributors.

Dave Plumby graduated from Linsly in 1972. He proceeded on to a distinguished undergraduate career at Notre Dame, after which he earned an MBA at Chicago's Loyola University. He was a rising young executive in the steel industry when he realized he did not care for the work. Wondering if there might be a place for him at Linsly, he was told by a sympathetic DiOrio that while there were no open positions, perhaps one might be created. Plumby thus began the 1982–83 school year doing odd jobs for the development office staff, writing an occasional piece for the alumni magazine and filling in as a typing instructor. It was not long before observant colleagues saw that his gifts might be put to more productive use, and a year hence he began teaching a new Linsly course in economics as well as assisting in the football and track programs. He would go on to replace Eudie Joseph as head track coach. Today Plumby serves the school as dean of students and director of the boarding program. In both roles, he administers disciplinary consequences, and his thoughtfulness and fairness in doing so have been deeply appreciated by the student body.

58 Dave Plumby, Dean of Students, circa 1995

59 Dr. David Mallow, Chairman of the Science Department, circa 2013

In 1984 the grand master of Linsly's science program, David Mallow, had just completed his PhD in biology from the University of Georgia. Needing a job, but hoping to find one in New York, he tentatively accepted DiOrio's offer to teach biology while, presumably, he would scan the horizon for openings at the university level. Thirty years later, Mallow is the thoroughly committed and much beloved head of Linsly's science program, teaching both introductory and Advanced Placement biology courses as well as other science electives. A passionate herpetologist, he has published a scholarly volume on snakes and maintains a substantial collection of living specimens in the basement of his campus home, stimulating both student interest and a measure of dread. An unfortunate incident in which a boa constrictor out for display locked its jaws around a biology student's shoulder and was reluctant to let go has become a permanent part of Linsly School lore.

60 Mark Landini (1986), Director of Alumni and Development, circa 2014

Newly graduated from Dickinson College, Mark Landini (Linsly, 1986) signed on as a counselor at the Linsly Outdoor Center in 1991, moving to the main campus the following year as a teaching intern. In 2003 he was named the school's director of development and alumni affairs, a post in which he has managed both to expand and deepen relationships with his fellow Linsly alumni. He has been instrumental in attracting major gifts, such as The Malone Family Foundation Scholars Program discussed in Chapter Thirteen, as well as in bringing sophisticated technology to the alumni and development operation.

The cadre of masterful veteran colleagues combined with a steady infusion of talented new ones provided a solid platform upon which to shape the contours of a revitalized school. In the minds of its graduates and their parents Linsly has proceeded into the new millennium with a remarkably clear mission. That mission can be seen as a distillation of values and practices forged at a succession of strong schools under strong leaders: Deerfield under Frank Boyden, Kiski under Boyden's protégé Jack Pidgeon, and Linsly under Pidgeon's protégé Reno DiOrio. Moreover, despite Linsly's seemingly protean structural changes over two centuries—from progressive Lancastrian Academy with a mission, to poor children to an all-boys military institute, to the coeducational college preparatory school of today—the school has been driven from its founding by Noah Linsly's testament that the school should always move "forward and no retreat."

"Forward and no retreat," apart from serving as the school's historic motto, is in essence the central lesson DiOrio inherited, first as a schoolboy, then as a schoolmaster at Kiski. When he began teaching and coaching at Kiski in 1965, he understood that he was part of a school culture in which boys did not quit teams when their expectations were dashed or their feelings were hurt. Boys did not drop classes or extracurricular commitments because their performance had fallen off or they had lost interest. Even more deeply, DiOrio understood that keeping commitments, whether doing so was immediately pleasing or not, was not just vaguely "moral," it was empowering for the children who endured. Children enjoined to stick with challenging commitments learned, even if they failed, what their personal limits were—and weren't. They learned, often, that they could achieve more than they thought, that talent and personal gifts, while always welcome, were less reliable resources than drive and effort. DiOrio's personal expression of the "forward and no retreat" sentiment was derived from Winston Churchill's famous exhortation to the boys of his alma mater, the Harrow School, in the autumn of 1941. Addressing the school at the height of Hitler's bombing blitz of London and other British cities, Churchill urged the boys "never [to] give in—never, never, never, never, in matters great or small—never give in."

DiOrio's emphasis on keeping commitments and following through was a recurring theme through his three decades of school leadership. It was likely to be the first point he would make in addressing students and parents in formal gatherings. Moreover, like other points he would stress with his colleagues and in school meetings over the years, his "never quit" message was derived from a larger vision of how schools are best run and how children best thrive within them. In this vision, it is best to keep matters simple, to express them in terms everyone, and certainly every child, can understand. Without being strident or hypercritical, DiOrio was wary of educational fads and trends, since ill-considered enthusiasm for them could impede a school's necessary business, which was to guide developing children to their full scholastic, physical, and ethical potential. In this regard DiOrio was determined to counter, or at least clarify, a number of educational buzzwords arising in the 1980s and 1990s. He was especially concerned about how children's "self-esteem" was being interpreted by popular educational pundits.

In an address to Linsly parents delivered on Parents Night in the fall of 1993, DiOrio cautioned that while "self-esteem is of great importance to the overall development of young people, [it] can never be given to someone by anyone." Challenging the assumption that a child's self-esteem could be imparted to uncertain and unhappy children through an unbroken stream of encouragement and praise on the part of parents, teachers, and other nurturers, DiOrio maintained that for both children and adults "self-esteem is the result of effort, perseverance, and realistic evaluation of one's ability. Self-esteem comes only through achievement and accomplishments." Seen this way, the developmental objective is to create a self-worth esteeming, not to heap well-meaning praises on a child stalled at some critical developmental task, such as mastering school challenges, developing essential skills, or making friends. DiOrio concluded, "My experience with young people has led me to believe that the quickest, as well as the most lasting, way for self-esteem to be developed is for a young person to try something that he is reluctant to try, and to enjoy some measure of success in that attempt."

DiOrio was equally concerned about how a seductive misunderstanding of the role of "happiness" in a child's life can impede development. In the same Parents Day address he challenged the notion that children experience anything like lasting happiness by having their whims and desires readily met. Genuine and lasting happiness, he proposed, was realized through effortful mastery of tasks, a point he said had been confirmed by Linsly students when asked to reflect on the teacher who had had the greatest impact on them. The results of this exercise, DiOrio reported, were that "the students, in essence, said the teacher that made them think the most, the teacher who expected the most, had the greatest influence." He added that, along with an appreciation for being stretched and challenged, students valued teachers who would make such demands in a spirit of positivity and with a sense of humor.

DiOrio would not waver from the conviction that children succeed more through trying hard than they do from a succession of easeful gratifications. "Success does not go to the brightest person," he would reflect in his final year as headmaster. "It does not go to the person who achieves the highest SAT scores, or the highest grades. Success goes to the individual who has learned to work hard, who has learned to persevere, and who has learned to adjust to frustration, failure, and disappointment that enters all of our lives at one time or another."

While perseverance and the inevitable taking of lumps was also central to the approach of DiOrio's headmaster at Kiski, Jack Pidgeon, DiOrio made an effort to strike a collaborative tone with Linsly parents, whereas Pidgeon was not beyond striking an accusatory note—to the extent of telling his audience at one memorable Kiski commencement that "you are the worst generation of parents in U.S. history." By contrast, DiOrio, in the course of Linsly commencements and other formal gatherings, was quick to thank parents for their care in nurturing their children, including the inevitable extra effort and commitments enrolling a child at Linsly entails. "How many miles did you log as personal chauffeurs for members of this group?" he asked, rhetorically, of the assembled parents at the 1999 Linsly commencement. "How many Little League baseball games and piano recitals did you watch... How many times after dropping your son or daughter off in the morning did you return to Linsly because of an assignment she forgot or his phys. ed. clothes? If you are parents of a boarding student, how many Fridays did you drive from Elkins, Clarksburg, Pittsburgh, or Charleston to Leatherwood Lane... only to reverse the process on Sunday? Of course the answer is too many—and if you could, I bet you would gladly start all over again."

In addition to periodically acknowledging the value of positive parental support, DiOrio offered a measure of parental guidance for responding to worrying cultural developments, ranging from children's increasing mobility and independence to their preoccupation with screened and other electronic diversions. In February 2006 psychologist Robert Evans, director of The Human Relations Service in Wellesley, Massachusetts, and a specialist in counseling school-age children and their families, was invited to address the Linsly parent body on what he called the "three pillars" of parental effectiveness: nurture, structure, and latitude. Among the observations Evans offered Linsly parents was his conviction that developing children do not thrive in the absence of reliable parental presence. Debunking the notion that a limited amount of "quality time" is sufficient from either parent, Evans stated that what children really need is "a great deal of low quality time."

In February 2008, just a year before he retired as headmaster, DiOrio invited another nationally distinguished psychologist and author, Dan Kindlon, to speak to Linsly parents about the findings of his new book, *Too Much of a Good Thing, Raising Children of Character in an Indulgent Age.* Kindlon's message—that excessive parental indulgence and permissiveness impede children's ability to achieve autonomy in adult life—could not have been closer to the heart of DiOrio's approach to child development. "Today's parents try too hard to create a perfect world for their children," DiOrio would reflect in 2009. "They try too hard to remove hurdles from their child's life, and they try too hard to protect them from disappointment. In doing so, parents rob their children of the very experiences most important to their development."

DiOrio's concern that Linsly students not be buffered from challenge, hardships, and disappointments does not derive from a hard-knocks or "boot camp" perspective in which children need to be "broken" so that they can be reconstructed in a socially desirable manner. Rather, he believes children are naturally resilient. Far from being permanently wounded by typical school setbacks and disappointments, students in his experience—he himself, for that matter—rebound quickly if treated consistently and fairly. This conviction of resilience was built into his personal approach to student discipline, summarized in a talk he gave in 2009: "I have made it a practice to always follow a confrontation with a student with an entirely different meeting with that student later. The message then becomes—you have made a mistake, but it's not the end of the world, let's move on."

Years before the mounting national concern about the educational and maturational costs of children being bound to their smartphones and other screens, the Linsly faculty began raising an alarm that students' engagement with televised and digital media—presently estimated at more than forty hours per week—was taking a toll on their health and physical viability. The faculty were equally concerned about the loss of relational skills and social judgment in consequence of so much electronic messaging and so little direct, face-to-face interaction.

Above all, DiOrio wanted parents and their children to be realistic with one another. Again addressing the Linsly parent body, DiOrio proposed that "when parents tell me their son or daughter tells them 'everything' that he or she does, I know I am in a conversation with unrealistic parents. Adolescence is a time for experimenting, and teenagers *do not* tell Mom and Dad everything. I always ask the parent who believes this, 'Did you tell your Mom or Dad everything you did?'"

Like Frank Boyden and Jack Pidgeon before him, DiOrio was equally concerned that expectations of children were neither unrealistically high or, worse, unrealistically low. "Set the bar low," DiOrio told Linsly parents, "and you won't get much. Set the bar high and they will meet the challenge. Some may fall short and require help—so be prepared to provide the help. Adults fail children by asking too little of them."

DiOrio's teaching and coaching colleagues have found it reassuring over the years that his educational views were not derived from any formulaic educational theory, but rather from closely observed experiences over time. He did not postulate children's resilience rhetorically; he seemed to *know* it. DiOrio likes to reflect on the natural exuberance of children at play before they enter adolescence—that is, their play outside the eyes of watchful adults. Children up through the age of twelve, he observes, establish rules and moderate disputes without adult intervention. Who benefits, he asks, when such children are supplied fancy uniforms, elaborate equipment, trophies, and banquets? What will be their expectations when they grow into their teenage years and beyond?

12 | Linsly On Course

Strengthened by consistent leadership and effective teaching in all departments, Linsly proceeded into the new millennium highly regarded throughout the region as providing superior preparation for competitive colleges and universities. Linsly was understood to be both scholastically rigorous and decorous. Linsly students were understood to behave respectfully, to try hard—and, in keeping with the school's ethos, never to quit.

The instructional climate and facilities the school enjoyed reflected the financial generosity and fiduciary wisdom of an especially committed board of trustees. Without the attentions and long service of Dr. Donald Hofreuter who would chair the board from 1975 until 2010, the extent and quality of the present school would not have been possible. Fittingly, a commencement prize was established in 2004 to honor "that member of the senior class who has been exemplary in his or her service to the school and community, in the tradition of Dr. Donald H. Hofreuter, Linsly Cadet Major, community leader, and long-time chairman of Linsly's Board of Trustees." Hofreuter's dedication to the school has been roundly shared by Robert Hazlett (elected 1970, long-serving board treasurer), Ogden Nutting (elected 1976) and his son Robert (elected 2002 and succeeding Hofreuter as chairman), Dr. Alan Fawcett (elected 1958), Judge Frederick Stamp (1976), Frances "Pinkie" Williams (1988), Joseph Gompers (1994), James McNulty (2000), James Dicke III (2000), Jim Squibb (1998), and Kevin Stevick (2007), currently chairman of the board.

From the early 1980s forward, DiOrio and the board presided over the gradual addition of needed facilities, beginning with a new boys' dormitory, East Hall (1983), and, with the advent of coeducation in 1988, a new dormitory for girls, West Hall. West Hall would be renamed Yost Hall in 2004 in acknowledgment of the generous support provided by Eugene and Prudence Yost. In 2007 East Hall was rededicated as Dicke Hall in recognition of the continuing support on the part of three generations of the Dicke family, including former Linsly students James Dicke III and his sister Jennifer. In 1992 a substantial gift to Linsly's $2.5 million capital campaign from Mrs. Joan Corson, nee Stifel, in honor of the Stifel family's continuing connection to the school, enabled construction to begin on a badly needed new recreational facility, dedicated the following year as the Stifel Field House. The new field house, appended to the Behrens Memorial Gymnasium, would provide additional practice and game space for both boys and girls. The field house was designed by architect E. M. Erwin, who had also designed the new boys' and girls' dormitories and was built by the Colaianni Construction Company.

61 Mrs. Pinkie Williams, Linsly's First Female Trustee

In the same year a generous benefaction from Anna Kuchinka enabled the school to acquire Hearnlee Place, situated directly across the lane from Banes Hall. Formally dedicated as Kuchinka Hall, the sturdy Tudor-style mansion was remodeled to house the admissions office, an infirmary, and administrative offices. The school's physical planning efforts were given an additional boost in 1996 by the sale of Old Main and surrounding property on the far side of Wheeling Creek to Kroger Foods, with the provision that the property be restored to Linsly in 2046.

Campus improvement continued apace as the stately Dallas Apartments building was acquired in 1997. Restored and refurbished to house alumni and development offices, the facility was renamed the DiOrio Alumni Hall in 2010 on DiOrio's retirement as headmaster. With the addition of the Williams Fine Arts Center in 1999, the range of arts offerings available to students was more than doubled. A complex of arts classrooms, performance spaces, and working studios, the new arts complex was the combined inspiration of Wheeling arts patron and Linsly's first female trustee, Pinkie Williams, and her architect son, Wick, who designed the conversion of what had originally been the Carriage House for the Dallas Apartments mansion. The arts complex would also serve as the first home of the newly conceived Linsly Archives, a brainchild of tireless Linsly benefactor Dr. Alan Fawcett (1937). Today Linsly's extensive archives are stored in a handsomely appointed museum housed on the first floor of a refurbished Carriage House on Knox Lane. The carriage house, originally attached to the Hearnlee mansion (now Kuchinka Hall), had become a separate property decades earlier and, given its adjacency to the campus, was a highly desirable acquisition for the school. That hope was fulfilled in 2003 when Wheeling businessman Richard Dlesk, father of two Linsly graduates, Richard (1976) and Randy (1988), and grandfather of Richard, Jr. (1997), Randy (2013), Cristian (2015), and Stephen (2017), negotiated the purchase of the house from the Wychoff family and presented the building to the school. Dlesk also provided funds for the extensive conversion of the ground floor to the museum and archives, the second floor serving as guest residence and conference center.

62 Robert Zaleski Standing Next to His Award-winning Self-portrait in 2006

Within the school's increasingly commodious facilities Linsly boys and girls were forging a new coeducational ethos as the number of admitted girls steadily climbed to parity with the boys. Earlier concerns that girls' efforts and voices would be muted by putatively more aggressive boys were largely put to rest as newly arrived coeds were quick to join and then to lead school activities. Cheryl Sprague, whose duties as academic dean of the Upper School included monitoring girls' progress through the school, feels that the ease in which Linsly girls found their footing could be attributed to the kind of girls who applied for admission, girls who *wanted* the challenge of breaking new ground. From the perspective of long-standing trustee Judge Fred Stamp, Linsly's admission of females was a thoroughly welcome development, a factor he believes led to the resurgence of faculty morale. Stamp's perspective was further informed by the experience of his son Andy (1999) and daughter Elizabeth (2002), both of whom were named head prefects as seniors and went on to study at Duke University and Brown University, respectively.

On the evidence of student publications of the late 1980s and 1990s, Linsly girls were not reluctant to make their voices heard. Even in the initial year of coeducation, 1988, when there were no girls yet enrolled in the junior or senior classes, female bylines began to appear in the newspaper and, soon after that, female names on the editorial staff. Moreover, female contributors to *The Linsly Line* apparently felt free to opine on what might formerly have been thought to be delicate matters. In the winter 1992 issue of *The Line*, for example, staff writer Christine Huffner expressed energetic support for a national policy of school-distributed condoms as a means to reduce unwanted pregnancies and socially transmitted diseases. While not addressing the more specific issue of such a policy at Linsly, Huffner urged her readers to heed the reality that "American children are having sex; it is a fact."

Both in the classroom and in extracurricular outlets there were clear signs that Linsly girls were eager and willing to make their views known. In the spring 1995 issue of *The Linsly Line* Jennifer Paulhus cast a critical eye on the American toy industry's propensity to perpetuate outdated female stereotypes. "Several products on the market encourage exclusively traditional female roles. One board game, Girl Talk, gives options for women's careers that included only mother, nurse, or homemaker." She further castigated Mattel for producing a Barbie doll programmed to utter, when squeezed, "Math is hard!"

However hard Linsly girls may have found their math and other subjects, they have managed to thrive scholastically. Since their admission to the school, more girls than boys have been named head prefect, a strong scholastic record being a key criterion for selection. More tellingly, Linsly to date has graduated four Presidential Scholars, all of them females. The Presidential Scholarship Program was established in 1964 to recognize unusual achievement on the part of graduating high school seniors, and the award represents the highest honor conferred on high school students in the United States. From all fifty states and U.S. territories approximately 3,000 top-scoring seniors on the SAT and ACT tests are vetted by the U.S. Department of Education to determine the top thirty male and female candidates in each state. About 3,000 students are invited to submit their school achievements and essays, which are reviewed before the selection of 500 semifinalists are put forward to a White House Commission on Presidential Scholars who then determine the boy and girl from each state to be honored at a special reception hosted by the President in June.

Linsly On Course

89

Linsly's Four Presidential Scholars

63 1993 Presidential Scholar, Kate Bodkin, with President Clinton

64 2000 Presidential Scholar, Elizabeth Paulhus, with President Clinton

65 2001 Presidential Scholar, Ashley Mulroy, with President Bush

66 2003 Presidential Scholar, Erin Morgan, with Secretary of Education Rod Paige

Linsly's first Presidential Scholar was Kate Bodkin (1993), a girl Headmaster DiOrio reckons may have been "the brightest student I have ever known." Kate would go on to study at Princeton University. In 2000 senior Liz Paulhus, the younger sister of Jennifer cited previously, became Linsly's second Presidential Scholar, matriculating to Boston College. Liz was followed by Ashley Mulroy (2001), who for two years conducted a groundbreaking study of animal-deposited antibiotics in the region's streams. Ashley would go on to explore her scientific interests at Harvard. Erin Morgan, the top scholastic performer in her class, was named Presidential Scholar in 2003 and earned her undergraduate degree at The College of William & Mary. To place these Linsly girls' achievements in some perspective, it should be noted that most high schools in the United States, including many well-established independent schools, have not yet produced a single Presidential Scholar.

Perhaps even more telling than the girls' recognition as Presidential Scholars is the degree to which the depth and rigor of their Linsly scholastic program prepared them for the challenges they faced in college and beyond. Erin Morgan, for example, expressed an abiding gratitude to her Linsly teachers for the ease in which she was able to manage a very demanding science program at The College of William & Mary.

> Like many incoming college freshmen, I was nervous about my first week of college. . . How difficult would it really be to pass organic chemistry? Part of our freshman orientation included a lecture where college administrators and counselors discussed how many freshmen often struggle during their first year. . . I wondered if I would be one of those freshmen.

> But, within the first couple weeks of college I was well into the academic rhythm. The classes were challenging, but I was well prepared, and I believe this is one of the most important results of my Linsly education. My course workloads were comparable to my experience in high school, and I knew how to stay organized and manage my schedule. . . Because I knew how to manage my academics, I felt able to become involved in clubs, intramural sports, and community outreach programs, which definitely enriched my first year experience.
>
> I was also very thankful for the challenging set of AP *[Advanced Placement]* courses that I completed while at Linsly, including Calculus AB and BC, Psychology, and Biology. The credit I receive from passing those exams put me a full semester ahead in my undergraduate career and gave me the flexibility to plan a study abroad program *[in marine science]* during my junior year.
>
> The Linsly Outdoor Center (LOC) provided some of the most memorable and meaningful experiences I had outside the classroom in middle and early high school. Going caving, orienteering, hiking and camping increased my love and interest of the outdoors—a passion that has ultimately led to my career focus in biology.

From William & Mary Erin went on to complete a master's program in marine science at the University of Oregon, followed by further study and certification in Wetland Management at the University of Washington. Today she is a practicing marine research scientist with the University of Washington School of Aquatic and Fishery Sciences in Seattle.

A quarter century after entering the newly coeducational Linsly, Kate Bodkin (1993), the school's first Presidential Scholar, while acknowledging the depth and substance of her courses, reflects that the most durable impact of her Linsly years is a habit of continuing intellectual engagement, a quality she believes was instilled in her by teachers who themselves embodied those qualities. A 1997 graduate of Princeton with a concentration in Victorian literature, Kate went on to earn a JD degree from Columbia University Law School, after which she practiced as a litigator in New York City for eight years before moving with her family to London.

> Three teachers who really stand out in my memory are Frau *[Margaret]* Ragni, Mr. *[Dennis]* Hon, and Ms. *[Elizabeth]* Hofreuter. I believe these three stand out so much not so much because of the subjects they taught (though to be sure they taught them well) but because of the additional wisdom and insight they managed to impart along the way. From Mrs. Ragni, I learned the importance of continuing to learn long after my time in the classroom ended. . . From Mr. Hon I learned calculus, which, truth be told, I don't recall having used since the AP exam, but I also learned about taking different approaches to find a solution to a difficult problem, and not being afraid to have a little fun

while I'm at it. And from Ms. Hofreuter, whose Humanities class was really an introduction to a college-style seminar, I learned to participate in my own education; not just rote learning or memorizing the material presented, but bringing my own ideas to the classroom and learning from my peers as well as the instructor.

For Elizabeth Paulhus, too, it was the vivid presence and example of specific teachers that stimulated her, first to achieve scholastic success at Linsly, and then to meet the challenges in college and beyond. Linsly's year 2000 Presidential Scholar, Liz matriculated to Boston College where she concentrated on theology and history, followed by a Fulbright grant that allowed her to carry out social policy research abroad before returning to Brandeis University's Heller School for Social Policy and Management where she completed her master's degree. Today relocated back in Wheeling, Liz serves as a regional director for Catholic Charities West Virginia. In 2012 she cofounded Ohio Valley Young Preservationists, dedicated to preserving and restoring historic buildings and sites. From her Linsly school days she recalls with enduring appreciation three of her teachers.

> I was fortunate to have Mr. *[Robin]* Follett for my junior year of English. Even in graduate school, I don't think I ever had a teacher offer better criticism of my writing style and logic. He taught us to replace adverbs with stronger verbs, to find the counterpoints of our points and then to refute them if we could. . . Perhaps the most important lesson I learned from Mr. Follett was that criticism of one's work often improves the final product and should not be taken personally. . .
>
> I had Mr. *[Chad]* Barnett for several courses in his first few years as a teacher. I think he is probably the most energetic teacher I ever had. There was no way to sit in his classroom in Kuchinka Hall and not be fascinated by American history. . . However, the other two classes I had with Mr. Barnett were some of my favorite in my entire education. During my junior year he taught two semester-long courses: Postmodern Literature and Woman and Literature. These classes had only seven or so students and were run more like seminars I would have in college. We were exposed to Margaret Atwood, Thomas Pynchon, Angela Carter, Charlotte Perkins Gilman, and so many other writers whose works were unlike anything we had read before. . .
>
> Words cannot describe the effect *[Dennis Hon]* had in my life and in the lives of so many of my classmates. His amazing record of AP exam performances by his students for both AB and BC calculus is a testament to his teaching. He used humor to make sometimes dry subject matter entertaining and memorable. Our BC Calculus class performance of the original play/musical "How the Honch Stole X-Math" at the Christmas Concert was one for the records. But more than that, I think what stands out to me is how much Mr. Hon cared for his students, even after they had graduated. I always knew that

if I had an issue, I could talk with Mr. Hon about it and get his sage advice. For several years after graduation, a group of us met up every Christmas and had dinner with Mr. and Mrs. Hon and shared news of our lives.

Perhaps the strongest element of continuity as the school progressed from an all-male military institute to the coed college preparatory school of today has been students' broad and enthusiastic participation in interscholastic athletics. Despite the school's comparatively small enrollment among rival schools in their division of the Ohio Valley Athletic Conference (OVAC), Linsly boys and girls have over the years consistently fielded competitive teams and have won an outsize share of conference championships. While at Kiski, DiOrio enjoyed the athletic rivalries among a number of strong independent schools, loosely organized as the Interstate Prep School League (IPSL), consisting of Kiski; Shady Side Academy in Pittsburgh; University School in Cleveland; Western Reserve Academy in Hudson, Ohio; and The Nichols School in Buffalo. In 1980 Linsly was invited to join the IPSL, with the understanding that contests with other IPSL schools would be arranged to accommodate Linsly's OVAC commitments and while Linsly enrolls fewer boys and girls than any of their IPSL rivals, the Orange and Black have managed over the years to be competitive—and in some seasons formidable—matches for their prep school counterparts.

67 Linsly's Varsity Football Team, circa 1987

DiOrio, his athletic directors, and coaching colleagues worked to infuse Linsly's interscholastic sports programs with three essential values: disciplined play, sportsmanlike conduct, and spirited fun. Successful school teams, especially when they go head-to-head with traditional rivals, invariably infuse the larger school body with energy and spirit.

Such was certainly the case during the twenty-six seasons (1980–2005/6) Terry Depew was head coach of the football program. Ably assisted by coaches

Dave Plumby, Dan Buchwach, John Whitehead, and Jim Napolitan, Depew's 1985–88 teams posted a remarkable twenty-six-game winning streak, including a Halloween night, end-of-season, come-from-behind victory over Magnolia High School, clinching both the OVAC championship and Depew's first undefeated season. The following year, emotionally boosted by Willie Clay's seventy-eight-yard touchdown run back of the opening kickoff in a surprise 23–0 victory over previously unbeaten River High School, the undefeated Orange and Black won a second consecutive conference championship. Nor would the 1980s be the end of the glory days for Linsly football under coach Depew. The Orange and Black posted another memorable undefeated season (10–0) in 1996, highlighted by the passing of sophomore quarterback Robbie Plumby (1998) and sophomore speedster Eddie Drummond's stirring final-second touchdown runs. The 1996 championship season was made sweeter by the fact that the final four games pitted Linsly against unbeaten opponents, including cross-river rival Bridgeport, Ohio, in the season finale. With each team 9–0 entering the game, fans for both sides filled the stadium to capacity—despite subfreezing temperatures—two hours before the opening kickoff. Linsly boosters' enthusiasm was rewarded by a hard fought and ultimately satisfying 24–14 victory.

Year in, year out Linsly's interscholastic teams have been composed of ordinary, willing boys and girls eager for the camaraderie of competing in a favored sport. Gifted high school athletes like Willie Clay, whose collegiate and NFL achievements were discussed in Chapter Ten, have been the exception at Linsly. Another is Eddie Drummond (1998), a Pittsburgh boy who entered Linsly in the ninth grade with a reputation as an impressive sprinter. After a tentative start on Linsly's varsity football team as a freshman, he went on to become a standout ball carrier and receiver on strong teams in 1997 and 1998. Recruited by Joe Paterno to play for Penn State, Drummond distinguished himself as a tailback and wide receiver. He was drafted to play for the Detroit Lions in 2002 where as a rookie he was among the leading NFL kickoff receivers, averaging twenty-six yards per return. After five seasons with the Lions, Drummond joined the Kansas City Chiefs for the 2007 season.

When Ashley Battle (2000) applied to Linsly as a boarding student in 1996, the admissions staff was unaware that she had already established an impressive reputation as a basketball player in AAU competitions in Pittsburgh. But upon her arrival it was clear that she was the best female basketball player in the school. Over four years of outstanding play on Linsly's varsity teams—she set school records for points scored, rebounds, assists, and steals—Ashley caught the attention of the leading women's collegiate basketball programs in the country, including Stanford, Duke, Penn State, and the nation's perennial NCAA championship contender, University of Connecticut. In her senior year, mired in the process of determining where she would study and where she would play in college, DiOrio recalls offering Ashley what he believed was wise counsel. He proposed that Penn State would perhaps be best, as it was close enough to home that her mother could see her play and, while offering an excellent basketball program, it was less competitive than Connecticut's and she would stand a better chance of playing on the team—to which she looked her headmaster in the eye and said, "Mr. DiOrio, I am not afraid of not playing at Connecticut." More than unafraid, Ashley proceeded on to Connecticut where she started and starred on three successive NCAA championship teams and was honored in 2003 as the Big East Defensive Player of the Year. She graduated from Connecticut with a degree in marketing and economics and went on to play six seasons of professional basketball with the WNBA, first for the Seattle Storm and then the New York Liberty. Presently an executive at Fifth Third Bank, in 2013 she was named girls varsity basketball coach for Chartiers Valley High School in Pittsburgh.

68 Varsity Baseball Coach Gary Sprague celebrates his 400th successful game with his team in 2001.

Over time, schools' athletic programs tend to become characterized by the sustained success of certain team sports. Whether graced by excellent coaching or by felicitous infusions of strong players, reliably winning teams become part of a school's identity and ethos. While Linsly has enjoyed periods of dominance in nearly all of its sports programs, from the closing decades of the last century, through the millennium, no team has been more consistently successful than its baseball team. Not long after the cessation of the Civil War, baseball became the premier sport in Wheeling and in the region—and, not surprisingly, for the cadets of the Linsly Institute. Never, however, has Linsly baseball succeeded better—or longer—than under coach Gary Sprague who, closely assisted by Terry Depew, guided Linsly's baseball team from 1973 to 2006. As noted earlier, in the course of those thirty-four seasons, Sprague's teams compiled a remarkable 488–253 win-loss record while winning thirteen OVAC championships and seven Eastern Ohio Baseball League championships.

Strong athletic programs inevitably inspire talented athletes to play on, and it is perhaps unsurprising that Linsly graduates have gone on to play professionally.

Although none would break through to sustained Major League careers, a number of Coach Sprague's leading players came close. Shortstop and pitcher Ron Stephens (1985) was drafted directly out of Linsly by the Red Sox organization, then worked his way up to AAA-level play for the Chicago White Sox, Cubs, and Detroit Tigers. Kevin Tatar (1986), an all-American pitcher at Wittenberg, joined the Cincinnati Reds minor league organization, finishing his career with the Chattanooga Lookouts. Another pitcher, Heath Haynes (1987), proceeded from Western Kentucky University to the Montreal Expos where he appeared for two weeks on their Major League roster before returning to the minors. From Notre Dame, infielder Mike Cross (1987) joined the Baltimore Orioles farm system, as did pitcher Mark Seaver (1993) after graduating from Wake Forest. Seaver would go on to play AAA ball for Oakland. Rob Cook (1987) attended Florida's Joe Brinkman Umpire School after his graduation from Ohio State and appeared briefly as a Major League umpire.

At the bicentennial mark, Linsly's dominance in baseball continues under head coach Jay Cartwright who, with assistant coach B.J. Depew, has guided Linsly teams to seven consecutive lopsidedly winning seasons and to OVAC championships in 2009, 2010, and 2012.

WHEN HEADMASTER DIORIO addressed his new colleagues at the outset of the 1979 school year, he shared his hopes of working together to build a strong, distinctive school. In that vision Linsly would be comfortably and sustainably enrolled with a range of promising students who were willing to try and eager to participate in what the school had to offer. The school would be scholastically rigorous and athletically competitive. The school's overall tone would be "traditional" in what it expected from its students' personal appearance, conduct, civility, and effort. American schools, dating back from the first academies in the early republic, have long postulated the twin aims of developing both intellect and character. The charters of the two Phillips Academies, first at Andover and then at Exeter, made the relationship between those two commitments explicit: of the two scholastic aims—the promotion of goodness and the promotion of knowledge—the former must be dominant. In the 1781 deed of gift for the Academy at Exeter, New Hampshire, the school's founder John Phillips wrote that "while the disposition of minds and morals will exceed *every other care*, well considering that goodness without knowledge is weak and feeble. . . knowledge without goodness is dangerous." Most schools include in their mission statements some kind of commitment to character building, but few of them state that promoting character is the school's primary and governing value. Fewer still can demonstrate ways in which the concern for character is central to school practice. In this regard, Linsly under DiOrio's leadership has emerged as a highly distinctive independent school, one in which fairness, keeping commitments, and perseverance in the face of disappointments and adversity are not merely stated but *practiced* values on the part of students and staff.

Three decades into DiOrio's headmastership it was clear to all of the school's constituents that his initial hopes for the school had been substantially realized. The school now annually enrolled 400–450 boys and girls, 100 of them boarders. Classroom buildings, residences, and other facilities had been added and renovated to accommodate them. The school's scholastic rigor was demonstrated yearly in impressive college placements and strong student performance on standardized tests, such as the nationally administered Scholastic Aptitude and Advanced Placement examinations. The athletic program, discussed previously, was vigorous, competitive, and intermittently dominant. Despite the challenges forever on the horizon of a fee-charging independent school in an economically struggling region, it was roundly accepted that Reno DiOrio had largely succeeded in what he had set out to do.

DiOrio's abiding friendship with his former boss and mentor Jack Pidgeon had alerted him to a possibility he hoped never to experience: the dispiriting realization that one might have stayed too long on the job. Pidgeon's remarkable forty-six-year tenure as Kiski's headmaster had not ended happily. Although he had resolved in his retirement to maintain a suitable distance from school operations while his successor established his own leadership protocols, Pidgeon had been constitutionally unable to do it, with consequent friction and hard feelings on the part of his former supporters and those of the new headmaster. That dissonance has now been put to rest at Kiski, but DiOrio, who observed it closely, was determined that Linsly should undergo no such ordeal. In the fall of 2008, after months of deliberation with his family, with Don Hofreuter and other trustees, DiOrio announced his resignation as headmaster at the end of the 2008–9 school year. Reflecting back on his decision today, DiOrio feels he might happily have served five more years, or even more. "But I would much rather have stepped down five years too soon than six weeks too late."

DiOrio had been a daily presence in the school: in classrooms, in hallways, at athletic contests, at concerts and performances of all kinds. His signature greetings and gestures—none more affectionately regarded than the gentle twist of a student's ear—had become part of the texture of daily school life. The

69 Reno DiOrio, Headmaster 1979–2009. "Success is never final—failure is never fatal—it is courage that counts. Never, never, never quit."

force and clarity of his discipline was understood throughout the school, but so was his compassion and support. Alumni ties to the school had become spirited and strong over the course of his tenure, and many DiOrio-era graduates who went on to prosperous careers, along with grateful parents, made generous contributions to the school's successive capital campaigns and to targeted special needs. Over thirty years DiOrio had become a successful fund-raiser, an accomplishment not lost on the trustees during the deliberations about his retirement. In addition to the funds secured for building projects and renovations, the school's endowment grew more than fivefold over the course of DiOrio's tenure, from $2 million in 1979 to more than $19 million. Because of his willingness to continue serving the school in some capacity and the invaluable relationships he had established with Linsly alumni and friends across the country, it was determined that on his retirement he would assume a newly created post as president, with special responsibilities for fund-raising and deepening relations with alumni.

Inevitably students were surprised and apprehensive when the retirement of their headmaster was announced, reactions that quickly coalesced into a chorus of appreciation. The October edition of *The Linsly Line* featured an interview with DiOrio in which he was asked his perspective on what he had achieved at the school. His response was unsurprising, "I would hope students and faculty would have seen me as someone who made every effort to be fair. I hope I have convinced some students that hard work and perseverance can overcome just about anything. That has been the story of my life personally. . ." Senior Lauren Joseph's editorial in that issue of *The Line* emphasized that DiOrio's stewardship of the school was characterized by close attention to individuals and by sheer

70 Headmaster Chad Barnett with Students, circa 2010

presence. "There is no method of understanding a situation that is quite as effective as actually *being* there, and this is the approach Mr. DiOrio decided to take in his career as headmaster."

The choice of DiOrio's successor was informed in good part by a general consensus of the trustees that the school was agreeably on course, and thus there was no mandate for a dramatic change. Moreover, the presence of a remarkably accomplished teacher-administrator already in the school's ranks dissuaded the board from conducting an elaborate national search. Chad Barnett, Linsly's director of admissions and financial aid since 2004, had professionally come of age at Linsly. Reared in Connecticut and a Summa Cum Laude of Bethany College in English literature, Barnett first visited Linsly in the spring of 1996 in hopes of finding a teaching post while he decided whether or not he might pursue a career as a lawyer. While DiOrio had no full-time teaching positions to offer at the time, he was suitably impressed by Barnett's scholastic and athletic record at Bethany, where he had been a starter and captain of the varsity basketball team through its 1994 and 1995 seasons. DiOrio was able to carpenter together a teaching internship, with duties including dormitory supervision, three seasons of coaching, and filling in for teachers in the humanities when they were ill or called away.

Reflecting later, Barnett recalls how he became quickly inspired by the way Linsly teachers managed to "cultivate a diversity of talents in each student." He remembers watching Danny Buchwach, son of Athletic Director Dan Buchwach, sing and dance the lead role in the school's performance of the musical *Joseph and the Amazing Technicolor Dream Coat*, and marveling that the hard-hitting linebacker on the school's football team and the attentive student in his history class was able to be so uninhibitedly dimensional. Barnett also remembers being impressed by the latitude Linsly teachers were given to prepare and execute their classes.

The following fall Barnett was hired full time as a history teacher, dormitory master, and basketball coach. Despite a demanding curricular and extracurricular load at the school, he enrolled in an MA program in English at West Virginia University, completing the program in 2001, as he did at Bethany, with an unblemished 4.0 grade point average and Summa Cum Laude honors. Having now migrated from Linsly's history department to the English department, Barnett taught all five sections of sophomore English, while also coaching basketball and supervising, with his wife, the girls' dormitory.

Barnett's enthusiastic appetite for school life was acknowledged by successive appointments as assistant director of admissions (1999), director of summer programs (2001), and director of admissions and financial aid (2004). In addition to his mounting responsibilities on campus, Barnett found time to build study opportunities for Linsly students at his alma mater, Bethany College, and to serve as an adjunct professor of English at the college. In addition he made time to travel the country and abroad delivering learned papers on topics ranging from postmodern esthetics to contemporary educational challenges. With dozens of published papers to his credit, he was admitted in 2008 to a PhD program in education at the University of Pittsburgh, where he is presently completing a thesis on the role of traditional education in an increasingly technology-driven culture.

Impressive as his academic credentials and services to Linsly had become, Barnett, on his appointment as headmaster in March 2009, was quick to acknowledge the formative impact of DiOrio's mentorship. Three years into his headmastership, Barnett recounted to the author the moment early in his career when he was sure he could be a viable teacher at Linsly. In the course of trying to reach a very oppositional student who had that day acted out dramatically, Barnett and the boy were walking along a corridor of Banes Hall in heated discussion of the boy's lapses and Barnett's concerns about them. Barnett, as he recalls, was feeling woefully inadequate to the task when DiOrio who, unseen, had observed and overheard the exchange, approached Barnett and the boy and quickly engaged the boy's full attention. He told the boy firmly that his behavior and attitude were unacceptable and that he was to go to his locker, pack his belongings, and leave the school at once and, the boy assumed, forever. Looking back, Barnett had expected to be called out on his ineffective discipline but instead felt thoroughly supported. Moreover, to everyone's satisfaction, DiOrio managed to meet with the boy after his clarifying removal from the premises and to win a commitment to better conduct.

71 Headmaster Chad Barnett, Trustee Chairman Bob Nutting, Head of the 200th Anniversary Campaign Don Hofreuter, and Reno DiOrio, circa 2011

Throughout the winter and spring of 2008–9 tributes to DiOrio poured into the administrative offices of the school. The winter issue of *Linsly Today*, the school's alumni magazine, was dedicated to Reno's and Karen's services over the course of their three decades in Wheeling. Among the dozens of remembrances published was a sentimental acknowledgment from Dan Stephens

(2000) of the reassuring personal *presence* Lauren Joseph had noted in her *Linsly Line* editorial.

> I can remember walking into The Linsly School as a 7th grade student. I really didn't want to be there and thought that I just might not stay. Mr. "D" made certain that I felt like part of the school. It took me till Christmas to realize that I was going to remain a Linsly student. . . I can't imagine Linsly without Mr. "D." He is like the institution itself. From the greeting at the entrance in the morning to a knee-bending squeeze on the shoulders in the cafeteria, students know this man. . . Mr. DiOrio has been so instrumental in creating an atmosphere that made us feel like a family. When I played at Pitt, he always let me know he was watching. . . He never forgets "his students." [Mr. DiOrio], you are truly one of a kind—for me a leader, teacher, mentor, and friend.

Brad Wilson (1984) wrote in gratitude for a specific lesson in perseverance impressed on him by his headmaster and coach.

> Apart from my parents, Mr. DiOrio was a tremendous influence on teaching me not only right from wrong, but the value of hard work. He and I would work tirelessly on my throwing technique on the football field, all while I was trying to convince him that I shouldn't even be the quarterback. I didn't want the responsibility of that position. Mr. DiOrio recognized that and never gave up on me. No, I didn't go on to play football in college, but he taught me that you don't run from things that make you uncomfortable, that you stay in the fight and learn how to make yourself better. Something so simple literally changed me as a person. My wife Cathy and I use this lesson every day to share with our own children some of "life's lessons."

Ashley Battle (2000) who, as noted earlier in the chapter, did go on to compete in intercollegiate athletics, was equally appreciative of her headmaster's insistence that she be at her best.

> For me, Mr. D. was the missing father figure I didn't have in my life. He would always pull me aside to lecture me about how important it would be to keep my focus and great things would be possible for me on and off the court. As a matter of fact, he still lectures me to this day. I'm sure all of his students can picture him walking down the hallway with his hands behind his back, slowly kicking his feet out one by one, humming to his own beat. It's unfortunate that future Linsly students are not going to be able to encounter his stern grip around the neck or a good kick in the shin. For those of us who have experienced it, we thank you for the many bruises and for caring enough to get our attention.

Mike Yukevich was a schoolboy with DiOrio at Kiski in the 1950s. Later in life when he became a Kiski trustee, he came to admire DiOrio's work as a teacher, coach, and administrator. A decade after DiOrio departed for Linsly,

Kiski's venerable Headmaster Jack Pidgeon underwent a serious bout of cancer, and the board of trustees, of which Yukevich was now chairman, began looking about for a worthy successor. Who better, Yukevich reasoned, than Reno DiOrio?

> I contacted Reno as [our] obvious choice. I knew that Reno loved Kiski. . . and did my best to convince him to return. My efforts were wholly fruitless. Visiting Reno at Linsly has shown me the kind of relationship he has maintained with students and faculty. . . I have confidence that his new relationship [as President] will be most beneficial to Linsly, and I wish both Reno and his institution the best.

Headmaster-elect Chad Barnett's tribute recognized that the transformative impact of DiOrio's leadership resided not just in his ability to motivate students to master particular skills and disciplines, but in motivating them to try.

> Mr. DiOrio offers a uniquely American answer to the question—What does it mean to be educated? His answer centers not on academic mastery or esthetic development, but on the emergence of a disposition. . . By his measure the true mark of an educated person is resilience. The educated person knows that at some point life will chew you up and spit you out. Debating the circumstances of the chewing and the spitting will get you nowhere. The educated person knows that in life's toughest moments, self-discipline, self-control, and a commitment to never quit are the best guides to see us through.

The same issue of *Linsly Today* also paid affectionate tribute to the school's "first lady," Karen DiOrio. Thoroughly admired as a veteran teacher of middle schoolers, she was warmly cited by her colleagues for helping to create a

72 The DiOrio Family. In front, Reno with Rena, Karen with Cecilia. In back, Matt (1987), Chris (1987), and David (1986) with wife Ellen.

welcoming family atmosphere in the larger school. Physically active, fit, and adventuresome, Karen DiOrio had been inclined to refresh herself in ambitious physical challenges, such as hiking the Peruvian jungle en route to Machu Picchu, lost city of the Incas, and climbing Africa's Mt. Kilimanjaro. She has also been an active volunteer for her church and for an array of community service organizations in Wheeling. In the course of an interview with her conducted by the magazine staff, she was asked "What can you tell us about the headmaster that nobody else would know?" To which she answered, "How he has grown"—particularly the emergence of an affable, outgoing disposition from the "very quiet and shy" young man she met and married in Miami forty-five years prior.

The DiOrios were further honored at a formal ceremony held at the Stifel Field House on the evening of May 9. The guests who packed the hall included trustees, faculty, graduates, parents, and DiOrio sons David (1986), Matthew (1988), and Christopher (1988). Following a musical offering by the Linsly Chorus and Strings, Trustee Chairman Don Hofreuter invited a series of speakers to the podium. Judge Frederick Stamp began the proceedings with an appreciation of DiOrio from the perspective of trustee and parent. Judge Stamp was followed by an affectionate reminiscence from the wife of Lieutenant Commander John "Sandy" Pidgeon, former Linsly teacher and eldest son of Kiski Headmaster Jack Pidgeon. Her remarks were echoed and amplified by a parade of DiOrio's long-serving colleagues. Gary Sprague and Development Director Mark Landini reviewed the growth and improvement in the school's program over the course of DiOrio's tenure. Business Manager and Assistant Headmaster Terry Depew celebrated the depth of friendship both DiOrios brought to the Linsly community.

Headmaster-elect Chad Barnett remarked on the signature combination of toughness and warmth that characterized his boss's approach to school leadership:

> What is the source of all that toughness and conviction? Having spent my entire adult life working with Mr. DiOrio and having watched him almost daily during that period, I have concluded that the source is love. It might not have felt like love when he kicked you in the shin. . . or when you felt that claw of death on the back of your neck. . . Several years ago Mr. DiOrio was invited to join a group called *The 100 Headmasters*. Late one spring I asked the headmaster, "Isn't your 100 Headmasters meeting soon?" He replied, "You know, I decided to end my time with that group. I just can't justify being away from campus at this busy time of year." That same week Mr. DiOrio attended two baseball games, a softball game, a track meet, a tennis match, and made several late-night rounds through the dormitories. Sounds like love to me.

The evening's festivities were simultaneously lightened and deepened when David DiOrio (Linsly, 1986), shared his reflections on being the son of a "tough" headmaster. He recalled reassuring friends who expressed their dread of being called into the headmaster's office with a confession of what it felt like for him to go home every night after school. David made it clear that his father was an affectionately revered fixture in the extended family and that, as Chad Barnett had noted previously, his father's conviction and toughness were grounded in love—but whimsically suggested that there might be moments when his father might, well, lighten up:

> I would be remiss if I did not at least mention the significance and almost singular focus my father has placed on the twin principles of hard work and being tough. I would like to tell you a brief story as to the importance he has placed on these ideals. My wife, Ellen, and I have two girls; Cecilia who is almost six and Rena who is almost two. . . Well, a couple of months ago our family dog died and my father wrote our oldest daughter a short letter telling her how sorry he was to hear the news. I was reading the letter quietly before I read it to our daughter, and got about three quarters of the way through when I laughed and shook my head. . . My father had started writing this note in an effort to comfort my daughter but had evidently been unable to contain himself. At the three quarters mark—and remember this is to a five and a half-year-old little girl whose dog has died—he began to say that this was an excellent opportunity to work harder and get tougher. . .

Before inviting DiOrio to the podium for concluding remarks to the assembled guests, Hofreuter announced three new gifts to the school in honor of Reno's and Karen's combined service: an endowed scholarship and a speaker series bearing their names, plus the renovation and renaming of the former Dallas Apartments mansion as DiOrio Hall, which would house alumni and development operations, including Reno's new office as president.

The dominant note struck in DiOrio's farewell as headmaster was humility. His opening words were "I cannot believe all of you didn't have something better to do this evening. . ." The anecdotes he shared were drawn from highly particular moments in his daily life at school—a sixth grader's bounding down the hallway after a class DiOrio had visited to tell him that his fly was unzipped; phone calls from mothers of new fifth graders on successive days, the first asking him please not to twist her son's ear, however affectionately, as it might frighten him; the second requesting that he please include her son in any ear twisting as the boy did not want to feel excluded. Lightheartedness aside, DiOrio wanted to remind his listeners that the substance—and rewards—of school life lay in its particulars, not in grand schemes. The measure of Linsly students, and thus the measure of their teachers and coaches, was not their scholastic prizes and achievements, but in their continuing conduct. When asked in a published interview what she would do differently in her career at Linsly, Karen DiOrio had cheerfully replied, "Nothing!" Her husband would conclude his assessment of his thirty-years' service with a similar sentiment: "I have enjoyed coming to school every day."

13 | Linsly at Two Hundred

In October 2013 Headmaster Chad Barnett and Board Chairman Robert Nutting announced to the Linsly community that after eighteen years' service to the school, five of them as headmaster, Barnett would be leaving his post to assume the headmastership of St. Edmund's Academy in Pittsburgh, beginning July 2014. In parting, Barnett expressed his indebtedness to his Linsly colleagues and students for what they had taught him about the value of independent school life at its best. Nearing completion of his doctoral degree in administrative and policy studies at the University of Pittsburgh, Barnett determined that his personal center of gravity had migrated to that city and that St. Edmund's, a kindergarten through grade eight independent school with a mission to educate a diverse student body to high personal and scholastic standards, was agreeably continuous with his work at Linsly. In the half-year transition to new leadership, Assistant Headmaster Terry Depew agreed to oversee daily school operations as Interim Headmaster, while Barnett shifted focus to strategic planning and other institutional research directed by the trustees.

The search for Barnett's successor as headmaster was directed by Stephen DiCicco of the Educational Directions consulting firm.

73 Terry C. Depew, circa 1998, Assistant Headmaster, Business Manager and Interim Headmaster 2013–14

74 Linsly's Twenty-first Headmaster, Justin Zimmerman. From left to right: Interim Headmaster Terry Depew, Linsly Trustee and Head of the Search Committee Kevin Stevick (1980), Aimee Zimmerman, Justin Zimmerman, Their Two Children John Michael and Bridget, and Current Chairman of the Linsly Board of Trustees Robert Nutting, April 2014.

Scanning a national field of interested applicants, the search committee hoped to locate a school leader with a distinctive educational vision, but one compatible with Linsly's traditional rigor. After three months of vetting applications, conducting preliminary interviews, consulting with applicants' past and present colleagues, finalists were invited to the campus where they spoke to and heard from all constituents: students, faculty, staff, graduates, and parents. By mid-March a clear consensus was reached that Justin Zimmerman, dean of student life at Western Reserve Academy in Hudson, Ohio, was the right man for the job.

Zimmerman had been a rising faculty star first at the Culver Academies (founded 1894) in Indiana where he taught biology and helped to develop an integrated science program, then at Western Reserve Academy (WRA, founded 1826), a distinguished college preparatory school, today enrolling 400 day and boarding students in grades nine through twelve. WRA shares a number of features with Linsly. Both schools completed a successful conversion of an all-boys school to coeducation. Both schools enroll day and boarding students. Though WRA has no lower school division, both schools serve approximately the same number of children and are able to achieve a similar sense of community.

Zimmerman was just thirty-six when he accepted the offer to become Linsly's twenty-first headmaster, having already made a substantial mark at WRA. An energetic and imaginative teacher of biology and Advanced Placement environmental science, he received Culver's Major General Delmar T. Spivey

Award for outstanding teaching in 2005. Two years later he was honored by WRA's Keener Prize for teaching excellence. In 2008 he was elevated into the administrative ranks, serving first as director of studies and then as dean of student life, a post in which he was responsible for the orientation, discipline, and guidance of all students. As dean of student life, Zimmerman led a number of strategic initiatives, including the introduction of a new daily schedule that included an extended learning block. He worked with department chairs to alter curricular content and to strengthen graduation requirements. He led the school's initiative to create a student-faculty Honor Council, and he designed a new health and ethics program for entering freshmen.

A devoted family man, Zimmerman, and his wife Aimee, have two children: a son, John Michael (nine), and a daughter, Bridget (six). In a letter to Linsly parents following his appointment he said that he had been deeply impressed by the sense of "community" so clearly shared by students, teachers, and parents: "My wife and I heard this word used in every conversation, and I think it speaks to the unity that is shared with all who are a part of Linsly. We also felt the pride students had when talking about their Linsly experience. From their stories in the classroom, on the athletic fields, in the dorm, or on stage, students know the great honor it is to be at Linsly."

Asked by the search committee to share his educational philosophy, Zimmerman opined that "teachers are the heart and soul of every school. By sharing their passion, teachers will generate excitement and passion around fundamental concepts and ideas. . . Time spent investigating students' individual questions should take precedent over studying arbitrary content. Learning should be authentic. Real, complex ideas and materials should be at the heart of the curriculum. It has been shown that concrete experience is the most powerful and natural form of learning. Students deserve the most direct possible experience of the content."

Apart from locating a new headmaster, the search process also provided a timely incentive for the school to take a measure of itself as it entered its third century of continuous operation. Apart from being the oldest school of any kind in the state, Linsly in its bicentennial year could fairly boast a distinctive educational achievement. Sustainably enrolled with 440 boys and girls in grades five through twelve, the school's college placement record was enviably strong in the region. In addition to perennially favored—and eminently affordable—West Virginia universities such as the University of West Virginia, West Liberty University, and Wheeling Jesuit University, 2012 Linsly graduates matriculated to strong colleges and universities across the country, including Big Ten powerhouses like Ohio State, Penn State, and Wisconsin, as well as selective national institutions, such as Boston University, Case Western Reserve University, Dickinson College, Lehigh University, Wake Forest University, the University of Pittsburgh, and the University of North Carolina at Chapel Hill.

From the standpoint of past and present students and their families, Linsly's proven ability to prepare students for university-level studies and beyond, while important, has defined the school less than its distinctive ethos. Since the school's founding, and certainly in the course of its century of military tradition followed by the rigorous expectations established over the course of the DiOrio years, Linsly has been an unapologetically traditional school. While progressive in its open-minded consideration of subjects under study and in its embrace of student diversity, Linsly remains decidedly conservative in its expectations of student conduct and appearance. The academic program is, as indicated in *The Student Handbook*, a "strong, structured, *traditional* curriculum" in which a thorough grounding in basic skills precedes engagement in advanced and individually elected courses. Linsly students are expected to contribute whole-heartedly to the extracurricular life of the school. The athletic program and the range of clubs and activities are notably broad given the number of students enrolled. Thus, supported by the school's "no quit/no-cut" policy, students are assured of a chance to compete and to participate in favored sports and activities, and those activities are strengthened by the expectation that every student will serve.

The Linsly *Student Handbook* also maintains that "character development infuses every aspect of the Linsly experience" and that "students develop respected character traits and self-esteem by facing difficult challenges and working to overcome them." These stated intentions are, at the time of this writing, roundly endorsed by both faculty and students. Disciplinary process is straightforward. Demerits are given for lapses in conduct, with consequent work details and detentions assigned if too many demerits accumulate over the course of a grading period. More serious disciplinary measures, including suspensions from school and expulsion, are determined solely by the headmaster. Infractions meriting serious discipline include using or providing alcohol or drugs at school or school-related events, academic dishonesty, theft, and bullying.

75 Linsly Students in School Uniforms, circa 2011

Expectations of students' personal appearance are similarly straightforward. The 2013 *Handbook* states that, "conservative hair styles are to be worn," and lest there be any confusion as to the interpretation of "conservative," it is further specified that boys' hair should be "off the collar, not covering the ears, and neatly combed. Extreme or faddish styles are not permitted." Boys are expected to be clean-shaven, with no long sideburns, mustaches, or beards. Tattoos and piercings, which are "discouraged in general," are to be covered by clothes. Boys and girls alike wear school blazers with Linsly patches. Boys are to wear shirts designed to be worn with a tie. Khaki colored or gray trousers are allowed, but not denim; leather shoes, not athletic ones. The girls' dress code is similar. School-provided khaki pants may be substitute for skirts of suitable length. While there is some discretion as to neckwear and other articles of clothing during the school week, on Mondays and anytime students travel away from the school to perform or compete, the full Linsly uniform is to be worn. In addition to establishing a decorous tone in classrooms and in the school generally, Linsly's traditional dress requirements are a unifying factor in student life, as is the uniformity and rigor of the scholastic program each student is required to complete in order to graduate.

Linsly students must master a balanced program of arts, science, and humanities courses in order to earn their diploma. Boys and girls who enter the lower school are offered a sequence of classes in which the foundational skills and subject content prepare them for the rigors of the high school program. Beginning in grade five, lower school students receive graduated instruction in language arts, social studies, and science. The mathematics sequence proceeds from advanced arithmetic through introductory algebra and geometry. Students are introduced to Chinese, French, German, and Latin, and all students take required courses in physical education, health, and fine arts.

At the Upper School, prescribed courses tend to precede elective courses in each discipline. Diploma requirements include four successive years of English composition and literature, four years of mathematics, three years of a foreign language (French, German, Latin, or Spanish), three years of science, two of which must be spent studying biology and chemistry, and three years of social science, two of which must be spent studying world history and U.S. history. Students must also complete required courses in computer science, art appreciation, music appreciation, and one additional elective course in the arts. In addition to their classroom studies, students must pass physical education requirements each term either by enrolling in instructional courses or by participating on interscholastic teams. International students' scholastic programs are augmented by Transition to American Language and Culture (TALC) courses, as needed. In sum, the scholastic program is a solidly traditional college-preparatory sequence. Advanced Placement courses are offered in all disciplines, and Linsly students have tended to distinguish themselves on them.

76 The Linsly "Whistlers" Performing at the 2014 Extravaganza

Just as the breadth and success of the school's interscholastic athletic program is somewhat surprising given the limited number of boys and girls enrolled in the school, Linsly's extracurricular outlets are extensive. After-school and weekend activities include club meetings for history, math, classics, and modern language enthusiasts. There are clubs devoted to studying Shakespeare, information technology, multicultural understanding, and preparation for Model United Nations competitions. Students also devote after-school hours to yearbook preparation, to composing and editing the school paper, *The Linsly Line,* and the annual literary magazine, the *Linsly Review.* Students rehearse and perform in the annual all-school Extravaganza, in the school's band and orchestral concerts, and in musical and nonmusical stage productions. Linsly teams and individual students also participate year-round in a variety of national, state, and school-wide scholastic and arts competitions.

In the fall of 2013 the Independent Schools Association of the Central States (ISACS) completed its seven-year accrediting evaluation of Linsly's overall program with a list of heartening commendations. The team of visiting evaluators was led by Clayton Chambliss, headmaster emeritus of Kentucky's Sayre School, and composed of twelve administrators and teachers from Midwestern independent schools. Foremost among the commendations was an acknowledgment of Linsly's strong, shared sense of community throughout the school. The team was particularly impressed by the clear commitment to character education they observed in their exchanges with faculty, students, and parents. The visitors noted the openness with which Linsly's constituents addressed perceived concerns, also the shared energy and enthusiasm with which the school was preparing for its bicentennial observances. Finally—and forcefully—the visiting team commended the care with which prospective teachers were vetted and hired, resulting in what the evaluators found to be a remarkably committed and effective faculty: "hard-working individuals willing to share responsibility and care for the student body and for each other."

To these commendations the ISACS team added five general recommendations: (1) that the school's administration establish a formal process to review curriculum in each discipline and to share best practices, (2) that the Linsly faculty consider further collaboration between and among teaching disciplines, (3) that administrators focus on professional development opportunities for faculty both on and off campus, (4) that the school clarify its twin commitments to "tradition" and to "innovation," and (5) that the school put full resources and energy into the restructuring of its leadership team in light of the imminent retirement of long-standing administrators and the current search for Linsly's next headmaster.

77 Faculty Who Have Served Linsly for Thirty Years and More. Back row from left to right: Dan Buchwach, David Mallow, Ray Smith, Frank Wilson, Bill Brubaker, and Dave Plumby. Front row from left to right: Denny Hon, Terry Depew, Reno DiOrio, Gary Sprague, Cheryl Sprague, and Mike Church, circa 2014.

The depth of faculty commitment commended by the ISACS evaluators is due in no small part to the length of service and consequent perspective acquired by Linsly's most veteran teachers. In addition to the long-serving teachers and administrators cited in Chapter Eleven, there are currently five senior faculty with thirty or more years of service. They include Bob Fisher, English instructor and former English department chairman; Bill Brubaker, social studies chairman and highly successful swim coach; Dave Riethmiller, math instructor and girls' tennis coach; Mike Church, math instructor and boys' tennis coach; and Ray Smith, math instructor and former head basketball coach.

78 Faculty Who Have Served Linsly for Twenty Years and More. Back row from left to right: Jay Cartwright, Mark Zavatsky, Mark Dodd, and Dave Riethmiller. Front row from left to right: Nicoletta Villa Sella, Kelly Soloninka, and Lisa Welch.

A similarly committed cadre of veteran staff have served the school twenty years or longer, including Kelly Soloninka, who in collaboration with Frank Wilson has masterfully taught fine arts courses, while directing choirs and helping to stage the annual Extravaganza; Dr. Nicoletta Villa-Sella, chair of the foreign language faculty; Jay Cartwright, social studies instructor and varsity baseball coach; his wife Julie Cartwright (Linsly 1991), head of Yost Hall, a girls' dormitory; Mark Dodd (Linsly 1985), director of buildings and grounds as well as lower school head football coach; Lisa Welch, lower school foreign language teacher and high school forensics coach; Mark Zavatsky (Linsly 1983), math instructor and highly successful golf coach; and Jill Regan, lower school arts and sciences instructor and coach of perennially strong girls' soccer teams.

By standard scholastic measures, the ISACS accreditors found Linsly an admirably strong school. Financially, too, the school stands on solid ground, its 2013–14 operating budget of approximately $8,500,000 supported by $6,400,000 in revenues from tuition and fees, $830,000 from return on endowed investments, and $500,000 from annual contributions of alumni, parents, and friends of the school. With a projected total endowment approaching $19,500,000, the school was able to offer just over $2,000,000 in financial aid. The capacity to offer generous financial assistance remained a critical factor in recruiting students from an economically straitened region. Financial aid grants ranging from as little as $1,000 per year to a substantial proportion of a student's annual fees were awarded to nearly half of the students enrolled. Another crucial factor in the school's affordability is that its 2013–14 day tuition fee of $15,590 and $32,170 boarding fee were substantially below—by $5,000 to $10,000 for day students and by $5,000 to $15,000 for boarders—that of comparable independent schools in the central states region.

Given the critical need for financial aid, the school's mission received a gratifying affirmation in 2012 when the Malone Family Foundation awarded Linsly one of its coveted $2,000,000 grants to provide financial assistance to especially promising students. Designated Malone Scholars, throughout the duration of their school careers, recipients are required to demonstrate a need of at least 30 percent of Linsly's tuition costs, to show clear scholastic motivation, and to rank in the top 5 percent of their classes in their previous schools. With a few exceptions, Malone Scholarship grants have been awarded to a single school in each state. Schools so honored are typically not selected on their first application. Impressed, however, by the initiative taken by Headmaster Barnett and by persuasive documents compiled by Development Director Mark Landini and his staff, Linsly was chosen as the lone Malone Grant recipient from West Virginia and was able to name its first Malone Scholars for the 2012–13 school year.

WHILE THE ASSESSMENTS of outside evaluators such as the ISACS visiting team and the administrators of the Malone Foundation help to take the measure of the school at its bicentennial mark, there are other—and arguably surer—measures of a school's condition. On a gloomy, intermittently rainy day in November the author spent the late morning hours getting to know five seniors who were not altogether displeased to be released from classes in exchange for offering their views on how their lives had been affected by their experiences at Linsly. The boys and girls were moderate to strong scholars, day students and borders.

Zoe, whose mother and uncle were Linsly graduates, had entered the school as a seventh grader, was captain of the swim team, and was named a prefect her junior year. Peyton, a boarder, had come to Linsly from the Washington Beltway in the tenth grade. She was also a swimmer and served as president of a club she had helped to organize that helped out at an animal shelter in Wheeling. Alec had entered the school in fifth grade—a "lifer." He played soccer, ran track, wrote for *The Linsly Line,* and had been named head prefect his senior year. Jackie had come to Linsly in the sixth grade, following four generations of uncles who had been cadets of the Institute. She was captain of the girls' tennis team and an enthusiastic debater. Zeke, also a "lifer," entered Linsly in fifth grade from Martin's Ferry. He played on the varsity football and baseball teams and was named a prefect his senior year.

Within minutes of introducing themselves the seniors had relaxed and were eager to talk. Noting that they seemed remarkably comfortable with each other and with me, I asked them if the school had always felt to them comfortable and welcoming. The answer from all of them was a robust yes. Like a group of appealing eighth graders I had interviewed earlier, the seniors recalled how friendly their fellow students had been when they first enrolled, how teachers especially had made early efforts to get to know them personally. Peyton, whose three-year tenure at the school was the shortest in the group, said that the girls with whom she boarded had been quick to make her feel included. She added that the close friendships she had made in the dormitory helped ease her social passage into the larger school.

I asked them about coeducation. I told them I had been struck by the fact that all four of Linsly's Presidential Scholars had been girls and asked if certain areas of school life tended to be dominated by boys or girls. Alec, the head prefect, opined that boys and girls shared leadership about equally and contributed equally to school activities, adding, "It's a near perfect balance." All agreed that the student body was stimulatingly diverse. Zoe described the cultural mix of her classmates at Linsly as "a whole other world" from that of her high school friends at home, adding that wherever you were on the Linsly campus, you could hear languages of other countries spoken. Jackie agreed. "The diverse mix of people," she said, "is my favorite thing about Linsly." Zeke maintained that in his prior school in Martin's Ferry there was no diversity whatsoever.

The group was thoughtful in response to being asked if they thought studying at Linsly had "changed them." Zoe felt the school had definitely held her "to a higher standard" and that she had learned a sense of "self-management" she did not believe she could have mastered otherwise. Jackie added that her coaches and teachers always insisted on her being "her best." Zeke said that the rigor of what was asked of him had made him a stronger, more independent person. Alec recalled a remark Headmaster Barnett had made in the course of a meeting of prospective parents: "Linsly is a school where it is safe to be smart." "And," Alec said, "it *is* safe to be smart here." All agreed that the school's expectations of decent conduct and personal honesty had been formative. Asked the worst offense a Linsly student could commit, their immediate response was "academic dishonesty."

Inevitably, since they were seniors, I asked them what their future plans were. None of them had received definitive word yet from the colleges to which they had applied, although two had received provisional acceptances. Peyton, who hoped one day to work promoting animal welfare, was waiting to hear from Elon College and the College of Charleston. Zoe, who wanted to continue to swim competitively in college and after that to dedicate herself to early childhood education, was uncertain about where she would study next and applied to schools as unalike as Ashland University in Ohio and New York University. By contrast, Zeke was certain he wanted to attend Ohio State University where he planned to study business with a specialty in accounting. Jackie, who counted Linsly's diversity as her favorite feature, was enthusiastic about the possibility of attending Oberlin where she felt the commitment to diversity and appreciating differences was a defining feature. Alec intended to pursue a career in medicine and, among a cluster of highly competitive undergraduate schools to which he had applied, was hoping to be admitted to Harvard.

Twice during our extended conversation in the comfortable living room of the Dlesk Center, a member of the teaching staff stopped by to see how the session was going and to ask if either the seniors or I had "had enough." Even when we had continued on through what should have been the students' lunch hour, we had not "had enough." My initial impression that these were impressive, *likable* people who had given considerable thought to what their schooling had meant and what they planned to do with it only mounted the better we got to know one another. Though conservatively dressed to the letter of the school's code, complete with Linsly blazers and appropriate neckwear, there was an attractive ease about them. They were attentive to what I asked them and to each other, and they spoke with remarkable assurance and, at moments, eloquence.

They were going to miss Linsly, they assured me. I didn't say out loud but remembered feeling strongly *what lucky colleges to have such students*. I had not for a minute in their company sensed that they were conscious of any personal entitlements, that they were *elite*. Rather than expecting bright futures, they seemed appropriately respectful of the challenges that lay ahead—and of the effort it would take to meet them. Nor could there be any doubt that their resilience and eagerness to contend were in large part instilled in them by a very good school on the threshold of its third century of service.

79 Linsly students honor their school's 200th Anniversary by lining up in the shape of 200, circa 2014.

Note on Bibliography and Sources

As a genre, institutional histories can be forbidding to general readers. They are often commissioned, as this one was, to celebrate a milestone anniversary, but unlike similarly commissioned statues and portraiture, they do not remain long in public view. Shortly after their appearance they, being books, are consigned to library and archival shelves where they beckon browsers very faintly, if at all. For this reason I have tried to strike a brisk and lively tone, while maintaining, I hope, reasonable scholarly standards. The sources for most references to specific people and events are indicated in the text in order to avoid the encumbrance of formal footnotes and endnotes.

Few independent schools in the United States have taken such care to preserve and catalog their institutional records—or to do so in such a handsome facility. That the archives have achieved this quality reflects the vision of trustees Dr. Alan Fawcett (Linsly 1937), Pinkie Williams, and West Liberty State University historian Robert Schramm (Linsly 1952). First housed in the Williams Fine Arts Center in 1999, the archival material was installed as part of the Linsly Museum established in 2003 when the school acquired and renovated the Hearnlee mansion carriage house on Knox Lane. The Linsly archives have been maintained by retired Museum Archives Director Ron Miller (Linsly 1955), with the assistance of Dick Coury (Linsly 1952). Current alumni volunteers include Bill Wilson (1959), Eric Gartner (1970), and Robert Mull III (1974). All have been gracious and helpful to me. Ron Miller's patience in orienting me to the archives' catalogs and documents was invaluable in setting this history project in motion.

The school publications I consulted included yearbooks between 1908 and 1978 serially titled *The Cadet, The Major, At Ease,* and, 1979–present, *Linsly.* Also consulted were *Linsly Institute Publications, 1887–1921*; *Linsly Institute Catalogs, 1878–1919;* and *Linsly Institute Catalogs, 1940–1948.* Alumni publications consulted and cited were the *Linsly Alumni Newsletter,* 1982–1995, and *Linsly Today,* 1988–2005. Student life was referenced from a number of student publications, including *The Linsly Echo,* 1879–1881; *The Linsly Magazine,* 1911; *The Cadet,* 1930–1979; *The Linsly Line,* 1979–present; and *The Linsly Review,* 1983–2010.

Prior efforts to chart the school's history over the years have been essential to this one. Robert Schramm's 2003 pictorial history, *The Linsly School* (Arcadia Publishing) indelibly conveys the school's progress through a series of striking images, with commentary, of the school's campuses from the Lancastrian

Academy days at the corner of what is now Thirteenth and Chapline Streets, to its stately new quarters (briefly the West Virginia State House) at the corner of Eoff and Centre Streets, to the imposing Old Main at Thedah Place and finally to the extensive present campus at the terminus of Leatherwood Lane. Also helpful was West Virginia historian Philip Ross's 1994 monograph, "Forward and No Retreat: The Linsly Story." Given his family's seventy-two-year unbroken succession of Linsly students, Dr. Alan Fawcett (1937) is well positioned to reflect on the school's past in his "History of Linsly Military Institute," a typescript copy of which he kindly shared with me.

The history of the school does not cohere unless it is embedded in the history of Wheeling and its surroundings. I was helpfully informed by a number of books about the region, including Robert Schramm's *Wheeling Island, A Photographic History* (2006), *Wheeling Bicentennial, 1769–1969* composed by Clifford M. Lewis and others (1969), *Landmarks of Old Wheeling and Surrounding Country* by Charles J. Milton (1943), and *A Pictorial History of Wheeling* by Elizabeth and Robert Ainsworth (1977).

My understanding of the city's history has also been informed by the longstanding publication of its daily newspaper, *The Intelligencer/Wheeling News Register*, issued between 1852 and 1859 as *The Intelligencer* and between 1865 and 1903 as *The Wheeling Daily Intelligencer*.

The eulogy for Headmaster John Michael Birch was excerpted from the 1911 *Wheeling High School Record*. The account of Wheeling's Mold and Foundry's contract to produce the gates of the Panama Canal appeared in the April 30, 1911, edition of *The Pittsburgh Gazette Times*.

Plentiful, well-ordered, and accessible as the Linsly's archival material proved to be, it would have been impossible to convey anything of the quality of school life over the past half century without the comments and witness of living people. In this regard, too, Linsly's faculty and staff, trustees, and selected students could not have been more forthcoming and generous with their time.

Linsly President and Headmaster Emeritus Reno DiOrio's thirty-four-year perspective was of course essential to any consideration of the school in its post-military, coeducational condition. Still heavily engaged in alumni relations and development work, DiOrio over the course of 2012–13 composed a series of reminiscences, met with me to share school impressions and stories on each of my extended campus visits, and opened access to school records and Linsly staff. The clarity and speed of his responses to what I feared were too frequent questions were impressive—and warmly appreciated. Karen DiOrio was also generous in sharing her perspectives of lower school life and of the larger school community.

I extend bottomless gratitude to Cathy Depew, DiOrio's administrative assistant, to whom my requests for materials and other queries must have seemed to her at times like an additional full-time job. Like the DiOrios, Cathy Depew and her husband Terry—teacher, coach, business manager, assistant headmaster, and presently acting headmaster—bring a thirty-four-year perspective to past and present developments in the school. While he could not possibly have been busier, Terry has been quick and clear in recalling critical developments in the school's progress.

Lower School Director Gary Sprague, Linsly's senior master, has served the school for forty-two years and thus was able to share invaluable impressions of the transition from a military institute to the school's present form. His wife Cheryl, academic dean of the upper school, was a critical figure in the school's admission of girls in 1988. Both have provided thoughtful reminiscence through correspondence and in the course of campus interviews.

Development Director Mark Landini and his staff have graciously provided both general perspectives on the school's progress as well as documents and identifying information pertaining to distinguished alumni.

Busy as he was in the transition from his Linsly headmastership to his new post as headmaster of St. Edmund's Academy in Pittsburgh, Chad Barnett made time to see me both early and late in the course of composing the book. He shared with me several articles he had published on Linsly's place in West Virginia's educational complex and composed some eloquent reminiscence of his career from his first arrival as a teaching intern fresh out of Bethany College through his headmastership twenty years later.

That there is a Linsly to celebrate on the occasion of its bicentennial is in large measure due to the committed stewardship of its trustees. Dr. Don Hofreuter (Linsly 1950) graciously shared recollections gathered from his long service as board member (from 1968) and chairman (1975–2009), as did Dr. Alan Fawcett (1937)—cited previously. Helpful trustee reflections were also provided by West Virginia Federal Judge Frederick P. Stamp, Current Board Chairman Kevin Stevick (Linsly 1980), James Dicke III, and James McNulty (1960). Linsly 1959 classmates Jim Hazlett and Mike Murray contributed, respectively, a lively appreciation of English teacher Gordon Crawford and a poem recalling the spirit of the Institute in the late 1950s.

Alumna and Presidential Scholar Erin Morgan (2003) contributed a detailed account of how the Linsly program prepared her and her classmates for the rigors of college life and beyond, as did Presidential Scholars Kate Plemlich, nee Bodkin (1993), and Elizabeth Paulhus (2000).

I am also grateful to Andy Grimes (1944) and Mel Kahle (1953) for their schoolboy reminiscences in the Lockhart years.

Finally, I would be unable to make an honest account of my research into the culture of Linsly School without a decidedly nonbibliographical acknowledgment of Tony Figaretti and the attentive staff of Figaretti's Restaurant, located around a bend of Mount De Chantal Road from the Linsly campus. Apart from its delicious offerings and inviting atmosphere, it should be noted that one cannot proceed from the restaurant entrance to one's table, especially if one is in the company of a DiOrio, without a half hour's greetings and well-wishing from Linsly trustees, past and present parents, and graduates. Emanating at once the spirit of the school and the spirit of the city that contains it, Figaretti's has made a delightful contribution to this story.

Faculty and Staff for 2013–14 & 2014–15 School Years 200th Anniversary Celebration

Faculty Member	Department	Start Date	Years at Linsly	Coaching Responsibility
Sprague, Gary	Dean of the Lower School and World Language	1968	46	
Fisher, Robert	English	1979	36	
Depew, Terry	Asst. Headmaster/Business Mgr./Interim Headmaster	1979	35	
DiOrio, Reno	Director of Leadership Gifts	1979	35	
Brubaker, Bill	Social Studies	1980	34	Swimming
Wilson, Frank	Chairman of Fine Arts Department	1980	34	
Buchwach, Dan	Fine Arts/Director of Athletics	1980	34	
Smith, Ray	Math	1981	33	
Plumby, Dave '72	Dean of Students	1982	32	
Church, Hampton	Math	1983	31	Golf
Mallow, David	Chairman of Science Department	1984	30	
Sprague, Cheryl	Dean of the Upper School and English	1984	30	
Riethmiller, Dave	Math	1985	29	Tennis, Basketball
Zavatsky, Mark '83	Math	1987	27	Basketball, Golf
Villa Sella, Nicoletta	Chairman of World Language Department	1988	26	
Soloninka, Kelly	Fine Arts	1989	25	
Dodd, Mark '85	Director of Building & Grounds	1991	23	Basketball
Cartwright, Jay	Social Studies	1992	22	Baseball, Football
Welch, Lisa	World Language	1994	20	Forensics

(Continued)

(*Continued*)

Faculty Member	Department	Start Date	Years at Linsly	Coaching Responsibility
Barnett, Chad	Headmaster	1996	18	
Regan, Jill	Science	1996	18	Soccer
Hasis, Jeff	Director of Linsly Outdoor Center	1997	17	
Crews, Darryl	Social Studies	1999	15	Soccer, Softball
Depew, Benjamin '94	Chairman of Math Department	1999	15	Football
Gellner, Guy	Fine Arts	1999	15	
McCamic, Jimmie	Librarian	1999	14	
Corbitt, Kathleen	School Nurse	2000	14	
Hasis, Sue	Asst. Director of Linsly Outdoor Center	2001	13	
Moolten, Marjorie	Science	2001	13	
Colton, Sabin	Science	2002	12	
Landini, Mark '86	Director of Alumni and Development	2003	11	Football
Creely, Stacey	Asst. Dir. Of Adm./Dir. Of Public Relations	2004	10	
Cunningham, Penny	College Counselor	2004	10	Basketball
Cowart, James '98	Physical Education	2005	10	Football, Track
Olsavsky, Judi	Chairman of English Department	2005	9	
Holt, Bill	Social Studies	2005	9	
Newell, Rebekah	Social Studies	2005	9	Volleyball, Basketball
Brutto, Tiffany	World Language	2006	8	Forensics
Fries, Eric	Science	2006	8	Soccer, Lacrosse
Ochap, Sarah	English and Math	2006	8	Soccer, L.S. Track
Foose, Greta	Fine Arts	2006	8	
Loudermilk, Jennifer	English	2007	7	
Hall, Erica	Chairman of Physical Education	2007	7	Soccer, Basketball
Wallace, James '03	Social Studies	2008	6	Basketball, Football, Baseball
Tredenick, Melissa	Academic Dean	2009	5	Volleyball
Harvey, Damon	Fine Arts	2010	4	Cross Country, L.S. Track

Ochap, Carrie	Physical Education	2010	4	Basketball, Track
Valentine, Brian '02	Physical Education	2010	4	Wrestling, Football
Felt, Chad	English	2011	3	Baseball, Tennis
McWilliams, Colin	World Language	2011	3	Soccer, Basketball
Smith, Amanda	English	2011	3	Softball, Volleyball
Haning, Caty	Intern and World Language	2011	3	Tennis
Hobbs, Ryan '07	Social Studies	2011	3	Soccer, Basketball, Lacrosse
Reisinger, Aslynn '02	Director of Alumni Communications	2012	2	Basketball
Allison, Maggie	English	2012	2	
Gregory, Cara	Director of Technology	2012	2	
Swart, Taylor	Science	2012	2	Swimming
Smith, Kris '08	Intern, Athletic Trainer, Science	2012	2	Hockey
Hobbs, Katie '08	Intern and English	2012	2	Soccer, Track
Oberlin, Adam	World Language	2013	1	
Foley, Stephen	Science and Network Administrator	2013	1	
Pockl, Gerald	Math	2013	1	
Zitzelsberger, RJ '02	Director of Admissions	2013	1	Football
Wilson, Rebecca	Intern – Alumni and Development Office	2014		
Campsey, Catherine	Nurse	2014		
Clark, Katie	Trainer	2014		
Edinger, Bruce	Science	2014		
Haizlett, Ellen	Spanish	2014		
Kiedaisch, Chris	Intern	2014		
Martin, Greg	Math	2014		
Miazgowicz, Chelsea	Math	2014		
Willox, Chris	Intern	2014		
Staff				
Depew, Cathy	Administrative Asst. to the Director of Leadership Gifts	1980	34	
Volan, Tere	Administrative Assistant	1991	23	
Giovengo, Tom	Trainer	1993	21	
Stalder, Elizabeth	Administrative Asst. to Dir. Of Admissions	1995	19	

(Continued)

(Continued)

Faculty Member	Department	Start Date	Years at Linsly	Coaching Responsibility
Cartwright, Julie '91	Boarding Department	1995	19	
Duvall, Debbie	Bookkeeper	1997	17	
Sparks, Janet	Strings Orchestra	1997	17	
Bryant, Don	Woodshop Instructor	2001	13	
Lofstead, Chris	Administrative Asst. to Dir. Of College Counseling	2002	12	
Taylor, Dave	Asst. Soccer Coach	2006	8	
Hobbs, Karen	Administrative Asst. to Headmaster	2009	5	
Stevens, Megan	Cheering Coach	2009	5	
Depew, Tracy	Bookstore Manager, Boarding Department	2010	4	
Valentine, Brittany	Boarding Department	2011	3	
Allison, Judith	Piano Instructor	2012	2	
Redford, Phil	Director of Safety and Security	2013	1	
Museum Staff				
Eric Gartner '70		2010	4	
Robert Mull '74		2010	4	
Bill Wilson '59		2010	4	
Maintenance				
Vellenoweth, Scott		1984	30	
Rosepappa, Rich		1996	18	
Robinson, John		1997	17	
Turkaly, Bill		1997	17	
Lance Hunter		2003	11	
Schaal, David		2003	11	
Curry, Michael		2010	4	
Huber, Michael		2012	2	
Palmer, Kenny		2012	2	
Moreland, Bryan		2013	1	
Housekeeping				
Waites, Queena		1973	41	
Lucas, Darlene		1994	20	
Christy, Megan		2001	13	
Auten, Debbie		2005	9	
Plumby, Jamie		2009	5	

Spielvogel, Kathleen		2012	2

Aladdin Food Service

DeFazio, Michelle	Director of Dining Services	2012	2
Orban, Myra	Asst. Director of Dining Services	2013	1
Marlarski, Evelyn		1983	31
Bowman, Shirley		1985	29
Ebert, Bonnie		1997	17
Ray, Lisa		2004	10
Bachie, Crystal		2009	5
Klusovsky, Kay		2010	4
Albus, Chrissy		2012	2
Bland, Donna		2012	2
Kilmer, Chuck		2012	2
Liston, Larry		2013	1
Rose, Edward		2013	1
Wisvari-Weir, Susan		2013	1
Workman, Frankie		2013	1

LOC Dining Staff

Rice, Brandon		2012	2
Conti, Michelle		2013	1
Conti, William		2013	1
Lyons, Joan		2013	1

Index

A
A.J. Sweeney Company, 11
Ali, Mohammad, 58, 61n–62n
Auth, Frank, 44
Aviator, The (sculpture), xi, 21–22
    photo, 22

B
Banes, Richard, 49
Banes, Sophie, 48–49
    photo, 48
Banes Hall
    construction, 48–49
    conversion to coed, 67
    photo, 49
Barks, Herbert, 66
Barnett, Chad, xi, 73, 92, 113, 114
    background, 99–100
    photo, 98, 100
    resignation, 105
    tribute to DiOrio, 102, 103
Bates, Charles W., 20, 49
Bates, Charles W., Jr., 20
Battle, Ashley, 94–95, 101
Baylor School, as model for Linsly, 66
Behrens, H. Fred, 38
Behrens Memorial Gymnasium, 86
    photo, 37
Bell, Andrew, 3–4
Bell-Lancastrian method, 3–4
Benedict, Allan, 29
Bennett, Louis, Jr., 21–22
Bennett, Sallie Maxwell, 21
Bertschy, Louis, 20
Birch, John Michael, ix, 9–14
    photo, 10
Black Tuesday, 26
Boarding program, x, 32–33, 35–36, 53, 65
Bodkin, Kate, 90, 91–92
    photo, 89
Bond, Scott S., 59
    photo, 59
Boyden, Frank, 58, 62n, 80, 84
Boys Town, 43–44
Boys Town (movie), 44
Brinkman, H.W., 37
Brinkman, Joe, 96
Brisbane, John, 54
Brittingham, Jacob, 13
Brown, Henry, 40, 45, 53
    photo, 45
Brubaker, Bill, 78, 111
    photo, 78, 111
Buchwach, Dan, 78, 94
    photo, 78, 111
Buchwach, Danny (son), 99
Bush, George W., photo, 89
Byrum Construction Company, 49

C
Canfield, Jack, 70
    photo, 70
Cannonball Four, 43
Cartwright, Jay, 96, 112
    photo, 112
Cartwright, Julie, 112
Chambers, Earl, 18
Chambliss, Clayton, 110
Chicken Soup for the Soul, 70
Chorpenning, Harry, 51, 54–55
Church, Mike, 111
    photo, 111
Churchill, Winston, 81
City Beautiful Movement, 20
Clay, Cassius (Mohammad Ali), 58, 61n–62n
Clay, Willie, 64, 94
Clinton, Bill, photo, 89
Clutter, Don, 61, 72, 73
    photo, 72
Coeducation at Linsley, 65–70
Colaianni Construction Company, 86
Common School Movement, 6
Cook, Rob, 96
Cooper, Harry, 18

Corson, Joan Stifel, 86
Cowen, Lindsey, 30
Cracraft, Russell, 37
Crane, Donn, 29
Crawford, Gordon, 45–46
Cross, Mike, 96
Crutter, Edwin, 49
Curriculum, 10, 15, 107–9

D
Dadakis, Evan, 43
Dallas Apartments
    acquisition of, 86
    renamed DiOrio Hall, 104
Dalzell, Robert, 35
Deady, Daniel, 4
Depew, B.J., 76, 96
Depew, Cathy, 75
Depew, Terry, 71, 75–76, 93–95, 103, 105
    photo, 75, 105, 106, 111
DiCicco, Stephen, 105
Dicke, James III, 85–86
Dicke, Jennifer, 86
Dicke Hall, 85–86
DiOrio, Cecilia, 104
    photo, 102
DiOrio, Christopher, 57, 76, 103
    photo, 102
DiOrio, David, 57, 76, 103–4
    photo, 102
DiOrio, Ellen, 104
    photo, 102
DiOrio, Karen, 56–58, 76–77, 102–4
    photo, 76, 102
DiOrio, Matthew, 57, 76, 103
    photo, 102
DiOrio, Rena, 104
    photo, 102
DiOrio, Reno, vii, x, 42, 53, 55, 59–61,
    61n–62n, 63, 75, 77, 85, 93–95
    background, 56–58
    coeducation initiative, 65–66, 68, 70–71

DiOrio, Reno (*continued*)
   educational views, 80–84
   as fundraiser, 98
   legacy, 96–104
   photo, 76, 97, 100, 102, 111
   recruitment of minorities, 64
DiOrio Alumni Hall, 46, 86, 104
Dlesk, Cristian, 87
Dlesk, Randy, 87
Dlesk, Richard, 87
Dlesk, Richard, Jr., 87
Dlesk, Stephen, 87
Dodd, Mark, 112
   photo, 112
Drummond, Eddie, 94
Drury, Roger, 58
Durant, Will, 29

E
Earhart, Amelia, 29
East Hall, 85
Easton, Gigi, 52
Echo, The, 10–11
Emblen, Joe, 17–18
Erwin, E.M., 86
Evans, Robert, 83
Extravaganzas, 41–42, 110

F
Fairi, Joseph, 35
Fawcett, Alan, 46, 48, 85, 87
Fawcett, Brian, 46
Fawcett, Ivan, portrait, 46
Fawcett, Jane, 46
Fawcett, John, 46
Fawcett, Raphael, 18, 46
Fawcett, Ronald, 46
Fawcett, Timothy, 46
Fawcett, York, 46
Final Drills, 39–40
Fisher, Bob, 111
Flanagan, Edward Joseph, 43
Follett, Robin, 92
Fort Fincastle, 1
Fort Henry, 1–2
"Forward and no Retreat" (motto), viii, x, 3, 13, 80, 81
Fostoria Glass Company, 16
Franklin, Benjie, 51
Franzheim, Woodward, 49
Fritz, Robert, 37

G
Gilleland, James, 37
Gompers, Joseph, 85
Gore, Howard, 22
Graham, Christopher, 28
Grimes, Andy, 52
Grimes, Bill, 65

H
Haigwood, Douglas, 40, 42, 47, 52, 59
   photo, 41
Haigwood, H.D., 35
Haliburton, Richard, 29
Hansen, Mark Victor, 70
Hasis, Jeff, photo, 69
Hawkins, Jim, 52, 59, 66, 68, 72, 73, 76
   photo, 63, 67
Haynes, Heath, 96
Hazlett, Jim, 45–46
Hazlett, Robert, 51, 76, 85
Hearnlee Place, 86
Henry, Patrick, 1
Hofreuter, Don, x, 43, 55, 56, 58, 59, 61, 67, 70, 85, 97, 103, 104
   photo, 43, 61, 100
Hofreuter, Elizabeth, 91, 92
Holden, Guy, ix–x, 17 –19, 22, 23, 26 –32, 37, 51, 65
   photo, 29
Holden, Mary, 27
Hon, Denny, 72, 74, 91–93
   photo, 74, 111
Houghton, F.C., 50
Huffner, Christine, 88

J
Jarboe, Lester, 49
Johnson, Andrew, 47
Johnson, Emerson, 66, 68
Jones, Pearson, 37
Joseph, Eugene "Eudie," 61, 72, 73, 78, 79
   photo, 73
Joseph, Lauren, 98–99, 101
Junior college program, 23
Junior ROTC program, 54

K
Kahle, Mel, 52
Keith, David, 50
Kennedy assassination, 48
Kent State shootings, 50
Kiesler, Kenneth O., 55

Kindlon, Dan, 83
Kiski School (Saltsburg, Pennsylvania), vii, 56–57
Kitchen, Ralph Ross, 20
Kuchinka, Anna, 86
Kuchinka Hall, 86, 87

L
Lafayette, George Washington, 5
Lafayette, Marquis de, xi, 5
Lancaster, Joseph, 3–4
Lancastrian Academy, ix, 3, 5
Lancastrian method, 3–4, 6
Landini, Mark, 80, 103, 113
   photo, 80
Lees, Thomas, 4, 6
Levenson, Marc, 47
Lindbergh, Charles, xi, 22
   photo, at Linsly, 23
Linsly, Noah, viii, ix, 2–3, 7, 13
Linsly Institute
   accreditation, 38, 110–13
   African American students, 64–65
   as all-boys school, 8, 16–17, 25
   archives, 87
   athletics, 24, 37, 39, 68, 72, 93–96
   Banes Hall, 48–49, 67
   Behrens Memorial Gymnasium, 37, 86
   boarding program, x, 32–33, 35–36, 53, 65
   as coeducational school, 65–70
   curriculum, 10, 15, 24, 107–9
   Dallas Apartments, 86, 104
   Depression years, 26–31
   Dicke Hall, 85–86
   DiOrio Alumni Hall, 46, 86, 104
   DiOrio era (summary), 96–104
   disciplinary process, current, 108
   East Hall, 85
   Eoff and Fifteenth Street facility, 7, 8
   extracurricular activities, 110
   Extravaganzas, 41–42, 110
   faculty, 111–12
   Final Drills, 39–40
   financial aid to students, 112–13
   financial status, 26 –27, 30, 50, 112
   "Forward and no Retreat" (motto), viii, x, 3, 13, 80, 81
   founding, 3, 4
   grade school program, 23–24
   Hearnlee Place, 86
   junior college program, 23

Index

Junior ROTC program, 54
Kuchinka Hall, 86, 87
Lindbergh visit, 22–23
Merriman Hall, 33, 35
military program ended, 58–60, 63–64
as military school, 10, 32, 39–40, 55
Minstrels, 41
Mount de Chantal partnership, 10–11
National Association of Independent Schools admittance, 38
National Honor Society, 37
as national school, 36, 37
Old Main, 20–21, 28–29, 40, 86
photos
    100th anniversary celebration, 14
    200th anniversary celebration, 115
    baseball team, 95
    cadets, 12, 16–17
    classroom, 25
    drills, 39
    flood, 40
    football team, 93
    fourth grade class, 38
    girls soccer team, 68
    junior college students, 35
    Military Ball, 40
    oldest, 11
    Old Main facility, 21
    rifle team, 54
    students in uniforms, 108
    swinging bridge, 41
    "Whistlers," 110
prefectorial system, 64
Presidential Scholars, 88–91
punishment duty, 39, 50
renamed Linsly Military Institute, 69
Second Century Fund Drive, 20
sixties era, 48–55
Stifel Field House, 86
student appearance expectations, 109
student interviews, 113–15
Thedah Place, 20
at two hundred, 107–15
Weiss Hall, 35, 44, 47
West Hall, 85
Williams Fine Art Center, 86
World War II years, 32–36
World War I years, 13–18
Yost Hall, 85
Linsly Military Institute, name changed to, 32
    See also Linsly Institute

Linsly Outdoor Center, 69–70, 80, 91
Lockhart, Basil, x, 59
    background, 30–31
    headmastership, 35, 37, 38, 43, 47, 51–54
    photo, 30, 53
    resignation, 51
    vision for Linsly, 32, 33
Lukeman, Augustus, xi, 21

M

Mallow, David, 79–80
    photo, 79, 111
Malone Family Foundation Scholars Program, 80, 113
Mann, Horace, 6
Marsh, Mifflin M., 11
Marsh Wheeling Stogies, 12
Marsh Wheeling tobacco company, xi, 11–12
McAtee, Wendy, 69
McClure, John, 7
McColloch, Samuel, 2
McColloch's leap, 2
McGee, Alexander, 4
McGee, Archie, 37
McGraw, Ralph, 44
McNulty, James, 45, 85
    photo, 45
McPhee, John, 62n
Mechlenberg, George C., 23, 28
Mendelson, Gordon, 47
Merriman Hall, 33, 35
Military Ball, 40
Minstrel shows, 41
Mold and Foundry Company, 16
Montessori, Maria, ix, 4
Morgan, Erin, 90–91
    photo, 90
Mount de Chantal, ix, 7, 8
    joint activities with Linsly, 10–11
Mulroy, Ashley, 90
    photo, 89
Munn, Lucille, 52
    photo, 52
Murray, Mike, 47

N

Napolitan, Jim, 94
Naranch, Brad, 70
Nasmyth, John, 51
Nassif, Louis, 37

National Association of Independent Schools (NAIS), 38
National Honor Society, 37
National Road, xi, 2, 5
Nedved, Andrew, 25, 44
Nutting, Ogden, 61, 85
    photo, 61
Nutting, Robert, 85
    photo, 100, 106
Nuzum, Marion, 37

O

Odgers, Harry, 13, 16
Ogden, H.C., 19
Old Main facility
    construction, 20–21
    flood, 28–29, 40
    photo, 21
    sale, 86
Oliver, Howard, 43
Osmena, Maria, 36
Osmena, Sergio, 36

P

Paisley, Brad, 42
Panama Canal, 16
Paterno, Joe, 94
Patterson, Charles H., 15, 16
Paulhus, Elizabeth, 90, 92–93
    photo, 89
Paulhus, Jennifer, 88
Peabody, Endicott, 58
Pearl Harbor attack, 33–34
Pell, Ned, 44
Perin, Samantha, photo, 67
Phillips, John, 96
Phillips Academies, 96
Pickles (musical), 29
Pidgeon, Jack, vii, 56–58, 80, 82, 84, 97, 102
Pidgeon, John, 103
Plumby, Dave, 79, 94
    photo, 79, 111
Plumby, Robbie, 94
Potter, James, 28
Presidential Scholarship Program, 88–91
Presley, Elvis, 45
Price, C. Burl, 29, 30
Punishment duty, 39, 50

R

Ragni, Margaret "Frau," 75, 91
    photo, 75

Ramsay, Robert, 34
Reeves, Bob, 74
   photo, 74
Regan, Jill, 112
Reger, John, 42–43
   photo, 42
Riethmiller, Dave, 111
   photo, 112
Rogers, James, 37
Rooney, Mickey, 44
Rose, David, 64–65
Roszak, Theodore, x
Rownd, Tom, 50
R.R. Kitchen Company, 20

S
Salgado, Peter, 33
Salgado, Peter, Jr., 33–34
Salvador, Ron, 55
Salvatori, Tony, 43
Salzarulo, Raymond, 51
Schramm, Robert, viii, 4, 13, 27, 39, 43
Scott, John, ix, 7, 8
Seaver, Mark, 96
Seitter, Oliver, 27
Shellhase, Janice, photo, 67
Sigal, Ron, 50
Sill, Father, 58
Sincavich, John, 37
Smith, Ray, 111
   photo, 111
Soloninka, Kelly, 112
   photo, 112
Sprague, Cheryl, 69, 71–73, 87
   photo, 67, 71, 111
Sprague, Don, 72
Sprague, Doug, 72
Sprague, Gary, 71–73, 95–96, 103
   photo, 72, 95, 111
Sprague, Jaclyn, 72
Squibb, Jim, 85
Stamp, Andy, 87
Stamp, Elizabeth, 87
Stamp, Frederick, 61, 85, 87, 103
Standerwich, H.W., 17
State house of West Virginia, photo, 8
Steiner, Rudolf, 4
Stephens, Dan, 100–101
Stephens, Ron, 96
Stevick, Kevin, 64, 85
   photo, 64, 106

Stewart, P. L., 33, 35, 40
   photo, 32
Stifel, E.W., 19
Stifel Field House, 86
Stock market crash, 26
Strider, Robert, 29–30
Swalm, Harrison, 37
Swinging bridge
   photo, 41
   rebuilding, 47

T
Tatar, Kevin, 96
Thang, Ton Duc, 51
Thedah Place, 20
Time Out for Ginger (musical), 29
Tomahawk rights, 1
Too Much of a Good Thing, Raising Children of Character in an Indulgent Age, 83
Tracy, Spencer, 44
Truax, John F., 4

U
University School (Cleveland), vii

V
Victory Corps of Wheeling, 35
Vietnam War, 49, 51, 54
Villa-Sella, Nicoletta, 112
   photo, 112

W
Waldorf schools, 4
Wegner, Nicholas, 43, 44
Weiss Hall
   acquisition, 35
   demolition, 47
   wing added, 44
Welch, Lisa, 112
   photo, 112
Wells, Larry, 44
West, Harry, 35
Western Reserve Academy, 106
West Hall, 85
West Virginia
   first state house, photo, 8
   "floating capital" period, 9
Wheeling, West Virginia
   epidemic of 1833–1834, viii, 5–6
   flood of 1832, viii, 5
   Lafayette's visit, 5

   Lindbergh's visit, 22
   population, xi, 5, 6, 8, 11, 60
   pre-World War I, 16
   schools established, xi, 7
   settlement, 1–2
   shale, xi
   Wheeling Female Academy, ix, 7
Whitehead, John, 71, 94
Williams, Frances "Pinkie," 85, 86
   photo, 86
Williams, Wick, 86
Williams Fine Art Center, 86
Wilson, Brad, 101
Wilson, Cathy, 101
Wilson, Frank, 77–78, 112
   photo, 77, 111
Wilson, Gordon, 29
Wilson, Walter, 44
Wilson, Woodrow, 16
Woods, Frederick, 18
Wright, Stephen, 54
Wychoff family, 87

Y
Yoon, Jennifer, photo, 67
Yost, Eugene, 85
Yost, Prudence, 85
Yost Hall, 85
Yukevich, Mike, 101–2

Z
Zabek, Matthew, 37
Zaleski, Robert, photo, 87
Zane, Ebenezer, 1
Zane, Elizabeth, 2
Zane, Noah, viii, 2–6
Zanesburg, 1
Zavatsky, Mark, 112
   photo, 78, 112
Zimmerman, Aimee, 107
   photo, 106
Zimmerman, Bridget, 107
   photo, 106
Zimmerman, John Michael, 107
   photo, 106
Zimmerman, Justin
   background, 106–7
   educational philosophy, 107
   photo, 106

Author Biography

80 The Author, Richard Hawley, Speaking to Linsly Students in 1986

RICHARD HAWLEY WAS BORN IN 1945 IN CHICAGO. HE ATTENDED SUBURBAN public schools in Arlington Heights, Illinois, before attending Middlebury College, where he completed his BA in political science. He went on to graduate studies at Case Western Reserve University, where he earned an MS in management science and a PhD in political philosophy. He also studied theology for a year at St. John's College, Cambridge University, as an MA research student under the tutelage of the theologian W. Norman Pittenger.

In the fall of 1968 he began teaching at Cleveland's University School, an independent college-preparatory school for boys. He would go on to teach history, economics, philosophy, and English literature, while also serving the school as history department chairman, dean of students, director of the Upper School, and, from 1988 until his retirement in 2005, headmaster. In 1995 he was named the founding president of the International Boys Schools Coalition.

A writer of fiction, poetry, and literary nonfiction, he has published twenty-seven books and several monographs. His essays, articles, and poems have appeared in dozens of literary, scholarly, and commercial journals, including the *New York Times,* the *Atlantic Monthly, American Film, Commonweal, America Orion,* and *The Christian Science Monitor,* and are represented in many literary anthologies.

He has lectured extensively at universities, schools, and conferences in the United States, Canada, Great Britain, and Australia. He is married to Mary Hawley, a painter and fabric artist. They live in Ripton, Vermont.